973.0495 92

New

DEC 19 2007

■ THE NEW IMMIGRANTS ■

Vietnam

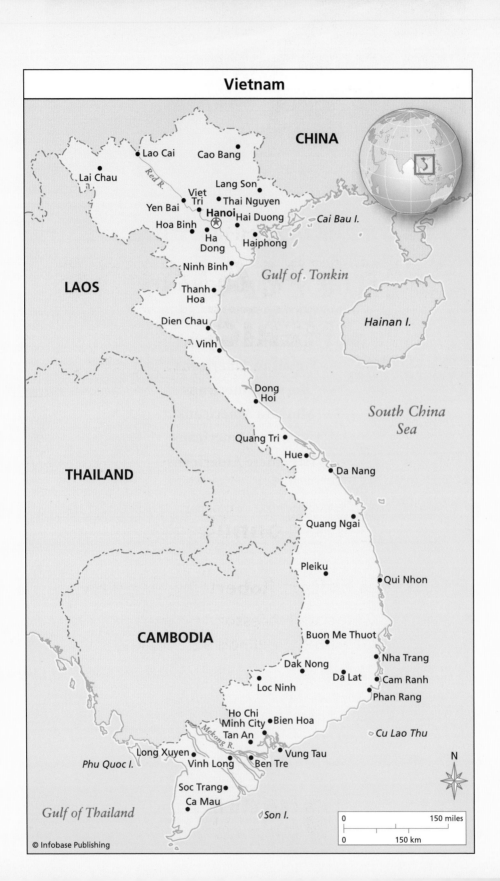

CHINA

Lao Cai

Cao Bang

Lai Chau

Red R.

Lang Son

Viet
Tri

Thai Nguyen

Yen Bai

Hanoi

Hai Duong

Cai Bau I.

Hoa Binh

Ha
Dong

Haiphong

LAOS

Ninh Binh

Thanh
Hoa

Gulf of Tonkin

Dien Chau

Vinh

Hainan I.

Dong
Hoi

South China
Sea

Quang Tri

Hue

THAILAND

Da Nang

Quang Ngai

Pleiku

Qui Nhon

Buon Me Thuot

CAMBODIA

Nha Trang

Dak Nong

Da Lat

Cam Ranh

Loc Ninh

Phan Rang

Ho Chi
Minh City

Bien Hoa

Cu Lao Thu

Tan An

Long Xuyen

Mekong R.

Vung Tau

Phu Quoc I.

Vinh Long

Ben Tre

Soc Trang

Ca Mau

Gulf of Thailand

Son I.

N

0   150 miles

0   150 km

THE NEW IMMIGRANTS

VIETNAMESE
AMERICANS

Liz Sonneborn

Series Editor: Robert D. Johnston
Associate Professor of History,
University of Illinois at Chicago

CHELSEA HOUSE
PUBLISHERS
An imprint of Infobase Publishing

Frontis: The Communist country of Vietnam is located in Southeast Asia. The majority of Vietnamese immigrated to the United States after the South Vietnamese government fell to Communist North Vietnam in 1975.

Vietnamese Americans

Copyright © 2007 by Infobase Publishing

Chelsea House
An imprint of Infobase Publishing
132 West 31st Street
New York NY 10001

Library of Congress Cataloging-in-Publication Data
Sonneborn, Liz.
  Vietnamese Americans / Liz Sonneborn.
     p. cm. — (The new immigrants)
  Includes bibliographical references and index.
  ISBN 0-7910-8787-5 (hardcover)
1. Vietnamese Americans—History 20th century. 2. Vietnamese Americans—Social conditions—20th century. 3. Vietnamese Americans—Biography.
4. United States—Emigration and immigration—History—20th centur. 5. Vietnam and immigration—Hitstory–20th century. [1. Immigrants—United States—History—20th century. 2. Immigrants—United States—Social conditions—20th century. 3. Immigrants—United States—Biography.] I. Title. II. New immigrants (Chelsea House)
E184.V53S66 2006
304.8'730597—dc22   2006008383

Series design by Erika K. Arroyo
Cover design by Takeshi Takahashi

Printed in the United States of America
Bang EJB 10 9 8 7 6 5 4 3 2 1
This book is printed on acid-free paper.

Contents

Introduction

Robert D. Johnston

At the time of the publication of this series, there are few more pressing political issues in the country than immigration. Hundreds of thousands of immigrants are filling the streets of major U.S. cities to protect immigrant rights. And conflict in Congress has reached a boiling point, with members of the Senate and House fighting over the proper policy toward immigrants who have lived in the United States for years but who entered the country illegally.

Generally, Republicans and Democrats are split down partisan lines in a conflict of this sort. However, in this dispute, some otherwise conservative Republicans are taking a more liberal position on the immigration issue—precisely because of their own immigrant connections. For example, Pete Domenici, the longest-serving senator in the history of the state of New Mexico, recently told his colleagues about one of the most chilling days of his life.

In 1943, during World War II, the Federal Bureau of Investigation (FBI) set out to monitor U.S. citizens who had ties with Italy, Germany, and Japan. At the time, Domenici was 10 or 11 years old and living in Albuquerque, with his parents—Alda, the president of the local PTA, and Cherubino, an Italian-born grocer who already had become a U.S. citizen. Alda, who had arrived in the United States with her parents when she was three, thought she had her papers in order, but she found out otherwise when federal agents swept in and whisked her away—leaving young Pete in tears.

It turned out that Alda was an illegal immigrant. She was, however, clearly not a security threat, and the government released her on bond. Alda then quickly prepared the necessary paperwork and became a citizen. More than six decades later, her son decided to tell his influential colleagues Alda's story, because, he says, he wanted them to remember that "the sons and daughters of this century's illegal immigrants could end up in the Senate one day, too."[1]

Given the increasing ease of global travel, immigration is becoming a significant political issue throughout the world. Yet the United States remains in many ways the most receptive country toward immigrants that history has ever seen. The Statue of Liberty is still one of our nation's most important symbols.

A complex look at history, however, reveals that, despite the many success stories, there are many more sobering accounts like that of Pete Domenici. The United States has offered unparalleled opportunities to immigrants from Greece to Cuba, Thailand to Poland. Yet immigrants have consistently also suffered from persistent—and sometimes murderous—discrimination.

This series is designed to inform students of both the achievements and the hardships faced by some of the immigrant groups that have arrived in the United States since Congress passed the Immigration and Naturalization Services Act in 1965. The United States was built on the ingenuity and hard work of its nation's immigrants, and these new immigrants—primarily from Asia and Latin America—have, over the last several decades, added their unique attributes to American culture.

Immigrants from the following countries are featured in THE NEW IMMIGRANTS series: India, Jamaica, Korea, Mexico, the Philippines, Ukraine, and Vietnam. Each book focuses on the present-day life of these ethnic groups—and not just in the United States, but in Canada as well. The books explore their culture, their success in various occupations, the economic hardships they face, and their political struggles. Yet all the authors in the series recognize that we cannot understand any of these groups without also coming to terms with their history—a history that involves not just their time in the United States, but also the lasting legacy of their homelands.

Mexican immigrants, along with their relatives and allies, have been the driving force behind the recent public defense of immigrant rights. Michael Schroeder explains how distinctive the situation of Mexican immigrants is, particularly given the fluid border between the United States and its southern neighbor. Indeed, not only is the border difficult to defend, but some Mexicans (and scholars) see it as an artificial barrier—the result of nineteenth-century imperialist conquest.

Vietnam is perhaps the one country outside of Mexico with the most visible recent connection to the history of the United States. One of the most significant consequences of our tragic war there was a flood of immigrants, most of whom had backed the losing side. Liz Sonneborn demonstrates how the historic conflicts over Communism in the Vietnamese homeland continue to play a role in the United States, more than three decades after the end of the "American" war.

In turn, Filipinos have also been forced out of their native land, but for them economic distress has been the primary cause. Jon Sterngass points out how immigration from the Philippines—as is the case with many Asian countries—reaches back much further in American history than is generally known, with the search for jobs a constant factor.

Koreans who have come to this country also demonstrate just how connected recent immigrants are to their "homelands" while forging a permanent new life in the United States. As Anne Soon Choi reveals, the history of twentieth-century Korea—due to Japanese occupation, division of the country after World War II, and the troubling power of dictators for much of postwar history—played a crucial role in shaping the culture of Korean Americans.

South Asians are, arguably, the greatest source of change in immigration to the United States since 1965. Padma Rangaswamy, an Indian-American scholar and activist, explores how the recent flow of Indians to this country has brought not only delicious food and colorful clothes, but also great technical expertise, as well as success in areas ranging from business to spelling bees.

Jamaican Americans are often best known for their music, as well as for other distinctive cultural traditions. Heather Horst and Andrew Garner show how these traditions can, in part, be traced to the complex and often bitter political rivalries within Jamaica—conflicts that continue to shape the lives of Jamaican immigrants.

Finally, the story of Ukrainian Americans helps us understand that even "white" immigrants suffered considerable hardship, and even discrimination in this land of opportunity. Still, the story that John Radzilowski portrays is largely one of achievement, particularly with the building of successful ethnic communities.

I would like to conclude by mentioning how proud I am to be the editor of this very important series. When I grew up in small-town Oregon during the 1970s, it was difficult to see that immigrants played much of a role in my "white bread" life. Even worse than that ignorance, however, were the lessons I learned from my relatives. They were, unfortunately, quite suspicious of all those they defined as "outsiders." Throughout his life, my grandfather believed that the Japanese who immigrated to his rural valley in central Oregon were helping Japan during World War II by collecting scrap from gum wrappers to make weapons. My uncles, who were also fruit growers, were openly hostile toward the Mexican immigrants without whom they could not have harvested their apples and pears.

Fortunately, like so many other Americans, the great waves of immigration since 1965 have taught me to completely rethink my conception of America. I live in Chicago, a block from Devon Avenue, one of the primary magnets of Indian and Pakistani immigrations in this country (Padma Rangaswamy mentions Devon in her fine book in this series on Indian Americans). Conversely, when my family and I lived in Storm Lake, Iowa, in the early 1990s, immigrants from Laos, Mexico, and Somalia were also decisively reshaping the face of that small town. Throughout America, we live in a new country—one not without problems, but one that is incredibly exciting and vibrant. I hope that this series helps you appreciate even more one of the most special qualities of the American heritage.

Note

1. Rachel L. Swarns, "An Immigration Debate Framed by Family Ties," *New York Times,* April 4, 2006.

Robert D. Johnston
Chicago, Illinois
April 2006

1

A New Life

Jade Ngoc Quang Huynh arrived in the United States in 1978.
He was 22. In his memoir, Huynh described his tearful re-
union with his brother:

> We arrived at O'Hare International Airport the next af-
> ternoon. Two Vietnamese working for ICM [International
> Catholic Migration] met us and brought us to American
> Airlines for our final destination of Memphis, Tennessee.
> We waited five hours at the airport, exhausted. It was the
> longest trip of my life.... As I got off the aircraft my heart
> bounced inside my chest; I walked through the gate. I saw
> my brother, my sister-in-law, and four nephews. We ran
> toward each other and embraced; we cried. For a few mo-
> ments we couldn't speak.[1]

Seeing his brother, whom his family had given up for dead,
was the culmination of Huynh's long struggle to escape his

home country of Vietnam. It was also the beginning of his new life in America.

A VIETNAMESE CHILDHOOD

When Huynh was a child, Vietnam had seemed an idyllic place, full of beautiful sights and sweet smells. With his 16 brothers and sisters, he grew up in An Tan, a small village on the Mekong River in what was then called South Vietnam: "It was a generous place for the people who lived there—most of them were farmers, and the land was flat and fertile. . . . People were everywhere—near the river, in the yard, in the garden and on the rice fields, happily chatting with one another wherever the conversation would lead."[2]

Throughout Huynh's youth, South Vietnam was at war with North Vietnam. An Tan was largely unaffected by the fighting, however, until 1968, when Huynh was 12. During a major offensive, soldiers who sided with North Vietnam stormed through An Tan. They were chased by helicopters manned by U.S. soldiers, allies of the South Vietnamese. The helicopters sent a rain of bullets and rockets into Huynh's house. Huynh survived, but his beloved little sister Luoi was not so lucky: "[W]e saw Luoi lying on the red tile floor, as if she were asleep among the debris . . . . I didn't have enough energy left in my body to wail, but my tears fell."[3]

Despite the war, Huynh was able to stay in school. He excelled at his studies and in 1974 traveled to Saigon, the South Vietnamese capital, to study literature at the university there. When South Vietnam lost the war a few months later, though, Huynh's life was plunged into chaos.

The North Vietnamese sent Huynh to a prison camp. Tortured and starved, Huynh struggled to stay alive, although his agony was so great that he often wished for death. Finally, after a year, Huynh managed to escape. Fearing the authorities would find him and send him back to prison, Huynh was determined to get out of Vietnam. He tried to flee three times. On his third attempt, he and his brother Lan set off in an old boat they had patched up. Braving lethal storms and murderous pirates, they managed to reach the coast of Malaysia.

There, the brothers joined other Vietnamese in a *refugee* camp. For eight months, they waited for a country to agree to take them in. After years of fearing his own death was near, Huynh could at last imagine a future for himself: "I dreamed of a wonderful world, my third country, wherever it would be. I would have a chance to go to school, to work, to do what I wanted."[4] At first, Huynh hoped to go to Canada. When he and

After the Vietnam War ended in 1975, many South Vietnamese fled their country for fear of being punished by the North Vietnamese for their role in the war. Thousands of South Vietnamese refugees left the country by boat and ended up in Pulau Bidong (pictured here), a refugee camp in Malaysia that at one time held 42,000 refugees.

Lan learned their brother Tuong had survived the war and was living in Corinth, Mississippi, however, they set their sights on America.

LEARNING TO BE AMERICAN

After Huynh and Lon were reunited with Tuong at the Memphis airport, they all headed by car to Cornith. For a moment, Huynh seemed to have found the wonderful world he had dreamed of: "The drive home on that foggy night took two hours. It was beautiful along the road, houses scattered about with faint light shining from front doors here and there. The air was fresh."[5]

Living in Tuong's crowded trailer, Huynh gradually learned the basics of American life. Tuong showed him how to use the toilet and telephone and how to turn on the television. Even going grocery shopping was an adventure: "Tuong taught us how to buy food and his wife explained how to get better deals buying large quantities and using coupons. I could not believe all the stuff the supermarket carried, and how cold [the air conditioning] was inside . . . . I felt as if we took a whole market home and the bill was $80."[6]

As the weeks went by, winter weather set in. Used to Vietnam's temperate climate, Huynh found the cold hard to adjust to: "The trailer was heated but I felt a new kind of cold that chilled my bones. I put some sweaters and blankets on and walked about. My nephew made a joke about me, 'You look like an old man, uncle!'"[7]

Even though he found winter uncomfortable, Huynh was delighted when snow began to fall: "We went out and I saw that everything was white, cold, tender. 'It's snow!' one of my nephews shouted. I scooped some off the bush, put it into my mouth, let it melt. I ran about to catch the snowflakes pouring down like cotton in the air. . . . It was the first snowy day in my life and it stayed with me."[8]

DISAPPOINTMENT AND DESPERATION

Not every experience Huynh had in Corinth was so positive. Soon after his arrival, Tuong took Huynh and Lan to the local high school to register for English classes. The counselor told them they were too old. He said they should forget about school and find a job. Huynh was heartsick: "I was disappointed, and knew we could not find a job if we didn't speak any English. I did not know what I was going to do with my life, because the dream of going to school was gone."[9]

Huynh and Lan were desperate to help out Tuong financially. They applied for assistance from the government, but were turned down: "I didn't know what the reason was. I felt humiliated and insulted because wherever we asked for help, everyone turned us away."[10]

Huynh finally found a job at a fast-food restaurant but drew little satisfaction from it. His supervisor made fun of him and called him names because he spoke little English. With Tuong's help, though, Huynh found an English tutor, so each day he became more fluent in his new language.

TO CALIFORNIA

Huynh's brother Lan became fed up with Corinth. He decided to head to San Jose, California, where he had heard there were funds available for job training. Once settled, Lan called Huynh, urging him to come, too. Lan was learning to be an electronic technician, a job that would pay far more than any Huynh could find in Mississippi.

Huynh was not excited about moving away from Tuong and his family. "[W]hy was it that I had to leave every time I met my loved ones?"[11] he wondered. Huynh knew, though, that he had to earn more money to help his Vietnamese relatives: "I had to be strong since my family [in Vietnam] was calling for help. I consoled myself by remembering that I could come back to visit and that I could call [Tuong and his family]. This was America and not Vietnam."[12]

In San Jose, Huynh took English classes and was trained to be a machinist. A year and a half later, he found a job as a machine operator, making more than twice as much money as he had made in Cornith. Working 12 hours a day, Huynh saved what he could to send to his family, still trapped in Vietnam. Huynh finally was able to arrange for his sisters, two younger brothers, and a nephew to come to America.

"WHY DID I COME HERE?"

Despite his progress, Huynh often felt miserable and angry. On a particularly bad day, he took his sister and her daughter to apply for government aid. They were told that the manager of the office did not "want any Vietnamese"[13]: "I was frustrated, insulted, and humiliated but didn't know what to do. I felt defeated. Sorry, niece, I thought, I cannot help you to receive a few free gallons of milk a month to help you grow. Why did I come here in the first place? I wished I could go home, to a place where at least my skin and culture, my morals and values were the same as others."[14]

Huynh decided he had to do something. He wanted to start over somewhere new, somewhere that he could maybe finally obtain the education he had long craved. With his nephew and two younger brothers, Huynh took off in an old car, looking for a place where he could make a fresh start.

They drove aimlessly, crossing the entire country, before finding themselves in Bennington, Vermont. The car began to buck, then it refused to start. Huynh took it as a sign. He and his young relatives decided to make a new home in Bennington.

SUCCESS AT LAST

Huynh found a job as a janitor and again started English classes. At the urging of a friend, he applied to several colleges to study

American literature. Huynh started to dream of one day becoming a novelist.

As the weather turned, Huynh became restless: "The winter was hard, the cold wind chilling my bones."[15] Then, he received word from prestigious Bennington College that it had awarded him a full scholarship. As he recalled, "The month was dreary, cold, and depressing, but I felt light."[16]

Huynh graduated from Bennington in 1987. He went on to earn a master's of fine arts from Brown University in Rhode Island and a doctorate from Cardiff University in Wales. He has since written *South Wind Changing,* the memoir that recounted his life in Vietnam and his journey to the United States, and co-edited *Voices of the Vietnamese Boat People: Nineteen Narratives of Escape and Survival.* Now an assistant professor of English at St. Lawrence University, Huynh published his first novel, *Family Wound,* in 2005.

Huynh's life is an incredible story by any measure, but it is not by any means unusual. Huynh is just one of hundreds of thousands of Vietnamese who fled their country for the United States in the last three decades. Many, like Huynh, have been able to build satisfying and prosperous lives here. Some, though, still struggle both financially and emotionally to get by. The story of each Vietnamese-American *immigrant* is unique, though all share a common theme—a desire to break away from a violent, sorrowful past and move toward a brighter, more hopeful future.

• Study Questions •

1. Where did Jade Ngoc Quang Huynh grow up?

2. How many times did Huynh try to escape?

(continues on next page)

(continued from previous page)

3. Why did Huynh want to come to the United States?

   ....

4. Why did Huynh move to California?

   ....

5. What college did Huynh attend?

   ....

2

The Home Country

L ong ago, there lived a dragon lord named Lac Long Quan. Taking the form of a human being, he married Au Co, an immortal goddess of the mountains. Their union produced 100 eggs. As the eggs hatched, 100 children emerged. Lac Long Quan and Au Co could not stay together long. Being a dragon, Lac Long Quan had to return to the ocean, and Au Co missed her mountain home. The two separated, each taking 50 children with them.

Vietnamese Americans still tell the story of Lac Long Quan and Au Co. They are honored as ancestors, the ancient father and mother of the people of Vietnam.

UNDER CHINESE RULE

The modern country of Vietnam (now officially called the Socialist Republic of Vietnam) lies on the Indochinese Peninsula in Southeast Asia. It forms almost an S-shape, broadest at the northern and southern tips and narrowest in the middle. The country borders China to the north, Laos to the west, and Cambodia to the southwest. To the east is the South China Sea.

Vietnam has a long and complex history, during which its borders and relationships with its neighbors have often been in flux. The Vietnamese trace the nation's origin back to about 2800 B.C. At that time, Hung Vuong, supposedly Au Co's eldest son, established the kingdom of Van Lang. According to legend, he and his descendants ruled for 18 generations as the Hung Dynasty. This dynasty came to an end in 258 B.C., when the last Hung ruler was overthrown.

The recorded history of Vietnam began in 207 B.C., when Van Lang was invaded and conquered by Trieu Da, a Chinese general. He declared himself emperor of Nam Viet, an area that included what are now southern China and northern Vietnam. The following century, the armies of China's powerful Han Dynasty invaded Nam Viet. In 111 B.C., the Hans made the area part of their vast Chinese empire.

For more than 1,000 years, present-day Vietnam remained under Chinese control. During this period, the Vietnamese were introduced to many new ways that had a lasting influence over their language, laws, government, educational system, and culture. Perhaps most influential were religious beliefs. While dominated by the Chinese, the Vietnamese were exposed to several new religions, including Confucianism, Buddhism, and Taoism.

These foreign customs had the greatest impact on the elite of Vietnamese society, because they had the most contact with the Chinese. The majority of the population, however, lived in farming villages, far away from the centers of power. Therefore, even with this constant exposure to Chinese ways, the Vietnamese, particularly peasants in rural areas, retained many of their traditional beliefs and practices, sometimes combining the old ways with the new in whatever way seemed best.

The Vietnamese also did not passively accept China's political control over their lands. Vietnamese history is full of stories of rebellions against the Chinese. The most famous was the insurrection led by two sisters, Trung Nhi and Trung Trac. The Trung sisters' revolt began in A.D. 39 after a Chinese official executed Trung Trac's husband for conspiring to overthrow the Han rulers. Together, the sisters organized an army to avenge his death. Amazingly, their force defeated the much more powerful Chinese Army. The Trungs declared Vietnam an independent nation, which they governed together as queens. The Trungs' rule, however, was short-lived. In 43, the Chinese again invaded Vietnam and took control. The Trungs refused to surrender. Instead, they chose death, committing suicide by jumping into a river.

Nearly 900 years passed before the Vietnamese were finally able to expel the Chinese. Led by Ngo Quyen, an army of nobles and peasants decisively defeated the Chinese occupiers. In 939, northern Vietnam became an independent state called Dai Viet with Ngo as its ruler. China, however, remained a threat. In 1407, the Chinese regained control over Dai Viet, only to be driven out again in 1428. Its independence restored, Dai Viet began expanding its territory to the south, reaching Vietnam's present size in about 1750.

A FRENCH COLONY

In the eighteenth century, the Vietnamese were again faced with a foreign foe. At the time, several European nations (Spain, England, and France) were using force to take control of other countries, especially in Asia and Africa. The process was known as colonization. Europeans sought to occupy foreign lands and turn them into colonies. They wanted to take over the colonies' economy, labor force, and natural resources and to send most of the profits derived from them back to the home country. Europeans also tried to subdue colonized populations and introduce them to European ways.

In 1777, the French military entered Vietnam. The French claimed they wanted to help rebelling peasants rise up against the elite ruling families of Vietnam, but in reality this proved to be little more than an excuse for the French to send an army to overpower the Vietnamese. With superior weaponry, the French defeated the Vietnamese and forced them to sign a peace treaty. It gave the French exclusive trading rights with the Vietnamese and access to their ports.

With this economic relationship in place, the French sent Catholic priests to Vietnam. The missionaries attempted to convert the Vietnamese to Catholicism. Resenting these outsiders and their influence, Vietnam's rulers began persecuting the priests and their converts. In 1858, the French used the murder of two priests as a pretext to invade Vietnam. After four years of fighting, they defeated the Vietnamese, but they did not take complete control of the country until about 1890.

The years of French rule were difficult for the Vietnamese. The French forced many peasants to leave their farms to work in French-owned mines and rubber plantations. The French then exported rubber and other Vietnamese-made products, retaining most of the proceeds for France. Furthermore, under French domination, the Vietnamese had few rights. They were not allowed to participate in their country's politics, and if they complained about the French, they faced harsh punishment, sometimes even death.

A small group of Vietnamese elites worked with the French and were educated in their language and customs. The new ways introduced by the French often directly contradicted Vietnamese traditions. Drawing in part from Confucianism, the Vietnamese believed that people should subordinate their own needs to the needs of their family, whereas the French emphasized the freedom of individuals to act as they choose. The Vietnamese traditionally valued a sense of harmony with nature. The French, in contrast, were eager to exploit natural resources for financial gain.

Ho Chi Minh, pictured here in 1950, became president of North Vietnam in 1945. Although both France and the United States were eventually driven out of Vietnam, Ho Chi Minh's forces fought the longest and costliest war of the twentieth century against foreign rule.

FIGHTING BACK

Just as their ancestors had resisted the Chinese, the Vietnamese resisted the French. Rebellions were constant, and they were often carried out by rural peasants. Some rebel leaders wanted to restore the old Vietnamese monarchy. Others wanted to establish a democracy or another type of government in Vietnam. All, however, wanted to overthrow the French and drive them out of their lands.

In the 1920s, an important rebel movement emerged around the leader Nguyen Tat Thanh, who later changed his name to Ho Chi Minh. His followers, the Viet Minh, formed the Vietnamese Communist Party in 1930. Communism is a political system in which the government owns all property and is supposed to distribute goods equally among all citizens. In practice, though, Communist governments have often become highly repressive and corrupt.

Many Vietnamese who joined the party had little interest in Communism, however. They were more attracted by the Communists' desire to free Vietnam from the French. As Father An-Phong, a Catholic priest who lived in northern Vietnam, explained:

> [I]n the beginning, most of the Vietnamese people did not know that the Viet Minh and Ho Chi Minh were Communists; that is why many of the seminary students left to fight with Ho against the French. Many people who joined the Viet Minh were not Communists; they viewed themselves as patriots.[17]

During World War II (1939–1945), the Japanese seized control of Vietnam from the French. Japanese rule proved brutal, especially in rural areas. The Japanese forced many peasants to farm cash crops instead of food. The Japanese destroyed or seized for themselves what little rice the peasants were able to grow. One woman, a Buddhist nun, described the horrors that followed:

People streamed into the cities looking for food, stealing whatever they could find, even taking it out of the hands of other people. Ravenous people overate and died of indigestion; the Japanese executed others for stealing, but many simply died of starvation.[18]

In the end, the famine killed about two million people.

BATTLING THE FRENCH

Amidst the chaos, the Viet Minh gained control over many rural areas, especially in the north. When the Japanese were defeated in World War II, Ho Chi Minh declared Vietnam's independence and won the support of a sizable portion of the population. The French, however, were determined to win back their colony. With aid from the United States and Great Britain, the French spent nine years trying to regain control of Vietnam by force.

Determined to crush the Viet Mihn, French troops savagely attacked anyone who appeared to be in league with the Communists. An Phong recalled his treatment by the French when, as a 10-year-old boy, he was arrested with some other suspects:

The soldiers led us to the military post. They forced us to push little bamboo boats for them that seated three or four soldiers. I was up to my chest and shoulders in the water. On the way, they beat me on the head with poles, and they put burning cigarettes on our cheeks. This was a favorite torture that they inflicted especially on the young women, and later they also raped them.[19]

The Communists played up such atrocities to bring more Vietnamese to their side, but the Viet Minh were also ruthless with their political enemies. As a result, many Vietnamese were repelled by both sides, as a man named Ngon from southern Vietnam explained:

When I think about the French and the Viet Minh, I see no difference. They did the same thing, and people were very scared of both sides. Both the French and the Viet Minh killed people in my wife's family. In my family the Viet Minh killed my first wife and my eldest brother.[20]

Finally, in 1954, the conflict came to an end with France's defeat at the Battle of Dien Bien Phu. International peace talks were held in Geneva, Switzerland, but the United States was very concerned about Vietnam's fate. It strongly opposed the Communist governments of China and the Soviet Union. U.S. officials feared Ho Chi Minh would emerge as Vietnam's new leader and establish Communism there as well. To counter Ho Chi Minh's influence, the United States backed Ngo Dinh Diem, a Catholic leader with little support among the Vietnamese people.

At Geneva, Vietnam was divided in two at the 17th parallel. To the north was the Democratic Republic of Vietnam, governed by Ho Chi Mihn. To the south was the Republic of Vietnam, ruled by Ngo Dinh Diem. Vietnam was reunited in 1956, after a nationwide election. The United States was not pleased with the arrangement. It refused to sign the Geneva agreement because it feared Ho Chi Minh would win the election. Largely because of U.S. resistance, the planned general election never took place, and Vietnam remained divided.

THE VIETNAM WAR

By 1961, tensions between the two Vietnamese governments were boiling over. Diem's regime in South Vietnam was threatened by Communist-led guerrillas known as the *Viet Cong*. The United States began sending U.S. troops to South Vietnam to assist Diem's anti-Communist government. U.S. officials, however, eventually lost faith in Diem's leadership. They helped to overthrow his regime in 1963, leaving South Vietnam in the hands of a series of military leaders.

During the administration of President Lyndon Johnson, the United States's involvement in the Vietnam War escalated.

By the end of 1967, there were nearly 500,000 U.S. troops in Vietnam. Even amidst massive bombing attacks, the Viet Cong were able to seize control of large areas in the south.

In January 1968, during the celebration of Tet (the Vietnamese New Year), the Viet Cong launched a major offensive. Briefly, they gained control of Saigon, the capital of South Vietnam. The Communist force also staged a brutal attack on Hue. It destroyed two-thirds of the city and killed about 10,000 people, half of whom were civilians.

During the Tet Offensive, although the Viet Cong suffered very high casualties, losing as much as half their fighting force, the campaign was in some important ways a victory for them.

Vietnamese refugees were forced to evacuate the village of My Tho during the Tet Offensive in 1968. Although the Viet Cong lost nearly half their fighting force, they briefly took control of Saigon and inflicted heavy damage on the city of Hue. More importantly, the Viet Cong's success convinced many Americans that the war in Vietnam was not worth fighting.

PHAN THI KIM PHUC: SPREADING A MESSAGE OF HOPE, PEACE, AND FORGIVENESS

On June 8, 1972, the South Vietnamese Army, on the advice of a U.S. military adviser, bombed the village of Trang Bang. The bombs spread napalm, a jellied gasoline that sticks to flesh and burns. One of the victims of the attack was a nine-year-old girl named Phan Thi Kim Phuc. Her body on fire, she ran down the street, screaming in pain.

The horrific scene was witnessed by news photographer Nick Ut. He took a picture of Kim, then rushed to help her. Ut sped her to the American hospital in Saigon. The doctors there did not expect Kim to survive. Even with burns covering half her body, though, the girl slowly recovered. After two years of treatment, Kim was finally able to return home. By that time, Ut's photograph of her was known throughout the world. It became one of the most famous images of the Vietnam War.

Following the war, Vietnam's Communist government exploited Kim's story to condemn the U.S. and South Vietnamese armies. Officials forced Kim to give interviews and appear in propaganda films. Feeling used by the government, Kim eagerly left Vietnam in 1986 to study in Cuba. Six years later, Kim traveled to Russia on her honeymoon. When her plane made a stop in Canada, Kim decided to stay there.

In 1996, Kim was invited to speak at a Veterans Day ceremony in Washington, D.C. Although eloquently recounting the pain and terror of her wartime experiences, Kim spoke of the need to forgive past wrongs. She also expressed her happiness with her new life in Canada, where she could at last enjoy freedoms unknown in Communist Vietnam.

With the help of the Vietnam Veterans Memorial Fund, Kim has since established the Kim Foundation International. This organization provides medical and psychological help to children wounded in war. Kim also continues to give speeches throughout the world, spreading her message of hope, peace, and forgiveness.

The American public had been led to believe the United States was winning the war, but after Tet, many Americans began questioning why U.S. forces were in Vietnam. As the public increasingly turned against the war, the U.S. government felt pressure to withdraw its troops from Vietnam. After lengthy negotiations, the United States, South Vietnam, and North Vietnam agreed to a cease-fire in January 1973.

The United States had removed itself from the conflict, but the fighting between the Vietnamese in the north and the south continued. The situation was certainly not unique in Vietnamese history. Over the past 4,000 years, the country had often been engulfed by violence and war. When this conflict ended, however, Vietnam would experience something new—a mass migration of its people, permanently fleeing from their beloved homeland.

• Study Questions •

1. Who were Lac Long Quan and Au Co?

2. How did 1,000 years of Chinese rule affect the Vietnamese?

3. Who were the Trung sisters?

4. What did the French gain by colonizing Vietnam?

5. When and why was Vietnam divided into North and South Vietnam?

6. Why did the United States send troops to Vietnam?

7. What was the Tet Offensive?

3

The First Wave

In the words that follow, a colonel in the South Vietnamese Army described the final day of the Vietnam War. On that day, Saigon, the South Vietnamese capital, fell to the North Vietnamese Army:

> As dawn broke on April 30, 1975, the last American helicopter took off from the top roof of the U.S. Embassy on Thong Nhat Boulevard. They flew up and off toward the southeast, the seaside, carrying with them the last American rear guard, leaving behind an unknown number of people, Americans as well as Vietnamese, who had been authorized to enter the U.S. Embassy compound in preparation to depart. They had waited their turn since the night before. Now the deadline was over. My family and I were among those left behind.[21]

In late April 1975, after Saigon fell to the North Vietnamese, many South Vietnamese scaled the walls outside the U.S. Embassy in hopes of finding a seat on one of the helicopters leaving the city. Despite being promised that they would be evacuated, many South Vietnamese were left behind to face North Vietnam's Communist forces.

For weeks before, the North Vietnamese had been staging a successful campaign in the countryside. About a million people poured out of the attacked areas. Traveling by car, by bike, and on foot, some headed for the coast. Others set out for Saigon. Soon, the grounds of the U.S. Embassy were flooded with people, all begging for the Americans to help them escape before the Communists arrived.

ESCAPING THE COMMUNISTS

As the Communists advanced, many people in South Vietnam feared for their lives. Among them were the 6,000 Americans living there. Also at risk were hundreds of thousands of Vietnamese, including people who had worked for American companies or for the U.S. government and soldiers who had fought in the South Vietnamese Army. Remembering the horrific murder of civilians in the city of Hue during the Tet Offensive, these Vietnamese had every reason to think they might be slaughtered by the Communist regime.

The rapid fall of South Vietnam had caught the U.S. government by surprise. U.S. officials had to scramble to come up with an evacuation plan. At first, the government decided to help only American diplomats and military personnel and a few thousand Vietnamese who had worked closely with them. Some U.S. officials in the military and the State Department, however, wanted to evacuate many more. These officials felt a moral obligation to their Vietnamese allies.

In the final days of the war and its immediate aftermath, Vietnamese refugees fled in three waves. The first included about 10,000 to 15,000 people and began about 10 days before the fall of Saigon. The second included about 85,000 refugees, who managed to escape in the last few days of the war. The third included 40,000 to 60,000 people, who left Vietnam on their own, most traveling by small boat or on foot, directly after the takeover. Approximately 130,000 of these refugees eventually made their way to the United States.

For the evacuees, the flight from Vietnam was harrowing. In a matter of days, their lives had been thrown into chaos. In the scramble to escape the country, they had little or no time to prepare. With few possessions or provisions, they took off on a journey into the unknown. Most had no idea how long their trip would take or even what their ultimate destination would be.

The escape was generally least traumatic for people who had close connections to U.S. officials. Many were able to board boats or helicopters, which took them to a fleet of U.S. warships waiting about 20 miles off the coast. Tran, a soldier for the

South Vietnamese Army, described how he relied on American friends to engineer his escape:

> I left Vietnam by boat, and headed to Hong Kong. I was helped by Americans who gave me American money to buy my ticket so that I could more easily escape Saigon. The ship I was on was a strong one, and I reached Hong Kong in five days. When I got to Hong Kong, I had an American sponsor which my [American] army friends had arranged for me. Since I already knew English, and since I had letters from my friends who were going back to live in the states, I did not have a hard time getting to America. I was very lucky.[22]

TERROR ON LAND AND SEA

Refugees who had to make their own arrangements usually had a more difficult time. Those who traveled over land did not always have enough food or water. In addition, along the exhausting trek, they were in constant fear of attack by North Vietnamese soldiers. Loc, who was nine years old when he left Vietnam with his family, described being stopped by North Vietnamese troops. After stealing the family's money and food, the soldiers separated the boy from his parents and interrogated him:

> I had been sitting alone for two hours when the soldier in charge came over and asked me if we had any gold with us. When I told him "no" he hit me with his fist and told me to tell the truth. He hit me three times and then placed his pistol barrel on my stomach and said that he was going to shoot me if I didn't tell him where the gold was hidden. I cried and could not talk. The soldier spit on me and walked away.[23]

After the soldiers let him go, Loc and his family finally reached Thailand. It took them two and a half years before they were able to enter the United States and settle in California.

Escaping by sea was hazardous, as well. Many of the refugees' boats were rickety and overcrowded. The passengers hoped to be picked up by a U.S. ship within a few hours, but often the boats drifted along for days, with no ship in sight, as those aboard became more and more frantic.

Some of these boats eventually reached the coasts of nearby countries, such as Thailand and Malaysia. Vietnamese were not always welcomed by the people on shore, however. One ship was at sea for six days before its passengers spied the Malaysian coast. A few younger people jumped out and began to swim to shore. They were met on the beach by angry Malaysians, who threw rocks and threatened them with knives. The swimmers had to turn around and head back to the boat. The same thing happened two more times, before the boat was finally able to land.

Refugee boats were also targets for Thai pirates. Mai, the daughter of a South Vietnamese soldier, was 14 when her family fled in a fishing boat. Crowded with 80 people, the boat wandered for three days, when a small pirate vessel overtook it:

> I did not know [at first] that these were pirates. But one of them grabbed me and forced me onto their boat along with some of the other girls. Four men took me into the boat and raped me over and over again. I tried to fight them, but they only beat me and laughed at me.[24]

The pirates held the girls for four days, then threw them into the sea. Mai and another girl were picked up by a boat of refugees; the others most likely drowned.

CAMP LIFE

While the refugees struggled for their lives, the United States scrambled to find a way to prepare for the arrival of more than 100,000 new immigrants. Congress eased the way for the Vietnamese's entrance into the country by passing the Indochina Migration and Refugee Assistance Act (1975). This act allowed

In 1975, the U.S. government passed the Indochina Migration and Refugee Assistance Act, which allowed Vietnamese refugees to enter the country without being subjected to the standard immigration procedures and provided $400 million for their resettlement. When they first arrived in the United States, these refugees were brought to one of four camps, where they were instructed in the ways of American life. Pictured here are refugees at Fort Chaffee in Arkansas, receiving instructions on the importance of dental care.

the Vietnamese refugees to enter the country immediately, by-passing immigration quotas. Congress also voted to allocate $400 million for their resettlement.

Almost overnight, the government also created four camps, which would be the refugees' first stop in America. The camps were constructed on military bases—Camp Pendleton in California, Fort Chaffee in Arkansas, Fort Indiantown Gap in Pennsylvania, and Eglin Air Force Base in Florida. At least initially, the camps were just temporary. Each was little more than a collection of large tents with about a dozen cots inside. There were also facilities for providing meals, showers, and clean laundry.

As time went by, the camps offered additional services. The refugees eventually had access to medical care and religious services, both for Buddhists and Catholics. To help with their transition into American life, refugees could attend English classes. Organized recreational activities and sporting events were also popular. With little to do, the refugees welcomed anything that would relieve their boredom.

Camp life was sometimes unsettling for these displaced people. Some found it difficult to adjust to American foods, which were far richer than the traditional Vietnamese diet of rice and fish. In addition, the camps often lacked needed supplies, such as blankets and jackets. Generally, though, life in the

Number of Immigrants Admitted to the United States from Vietnam, 1952–2004

Years of Entry	Number Admitted
1820–1951*	—
1952–1960	335
1961–1970	4,340
1971–1980	172,820
1981–1990	280,782
1991–2000	286,145
2001–2004	118,407

* Prior to 1952, immigration data for Vietnamese Americans was not reported separately.

Source: Department of Homeland Security Web site. Available online at *http://www.uscis.gov/graphics/shared/statistics/yearbook/2004/table2.xls*

camps was fairly comfortable. Even so, camp inmates were eager to leave, so they could start rebuilding their lives as Vietnamese Americans.

THE DISPERSAL PROGRAM

There were four ways people could gain their release from the camps: They could (1) resettle in another country, (2) return to Vietnam, (3) prove they were financially self sufficient, or (4) find a *sponsor*. By choice and necessity, nearly all refugees took the fourth option—finding a sponsor. A sponsor was an individual or a group that promised to help a refugee adapt to American life. The federal government contracted nine organizations to find suitable sponsors. The most active was the United States Catholic Conference, which matched sponsors with about half of the refugees.

In creating the sponsorship program, the United States hoped to settle the Vietnamese refugees throughout the country. There were some practical reasons for this *dispersal policy*. The government wanted to get the Vietnamese settled as quickly as possible, and the fastest way to find enough sponsors was to look for them across the nation. Officials also wanted to make sure that large numbers of refugees did not settle in one community. They feared that this could place financial burdens on the community and turn its residents against the Vietnamese. The government was aware that most Americans were already uneasy about Vietnamese immigration. According to a Gallup poll taken in 1975, about 54 percent of Americans did not want the United States to admit the refugees at all.

Some of these Americans saw the Vietnamese immigrants as an uncomfortable reminder of the United States's failure to win the Vietnam War. Others were afraid the Vietnamese would take their jobs. Still others had racist ideas about all Asians, so they were prepared to dislike the Vietnamese even before encountering any of them.

LIVING WITH SPONSORS

Because of the dispersal policy, agencies found sponsors in all 50 states. A few sponsors were family members. (Before 1975, about 15,000 Vietnamese were living in the United States. Most were foreign-exchange students and Vietnamese wives of U.S. soldiers.) The vast majority of refugees, however, were sent to live with American families.

Sponsors needed to meet a number of responsibilities for the refugees placed with them. They had to provide food, clothing, and shelter until the refugees were financially able to take care of themselves. Sponsors also taught refugees about American society. They frequently helped enroll children in schools and find jobs for adults.

Often, a church's congregation or a company's employees worked together to serve as a sponsor. Some American families agreed to take in refugees on their own. Being a sponsor required a good deal of time, energy, and money. All sponsors received $500 from the government, but this amounted to only about one-tenth of the funds needed to fulfill their duties.

Understandably, most Vietnamese families were very grateful to their sponsors. One woman who was resettled to a small town in Arkansas, recalled, "The Vietnamese people would never have done for complete strangers what they did for us. It was precious."[25]

On the other hand, refugees also found it stressful to live with their sponsors. They were often baffled by unfamiliar American manners and customs. The situation was worse for refugees who had no knowledge of English. Unable to ask their sponsors questions, they often felt isolated and confused.

For many refugees, however, the worst aspect of the sponsorship program was that it separated family members from one another. U.S. officials determined that only immediate family members would be resettled together. But in Vietnam, people usually lived in larger households that might also include grandparents, aunts, uncles, cousins, and other relations. In order to disperse the refugees throughout the country, the government often separated household members, settling them hundreds or thousands of miles apart. Many refugees deeply mourned the loss of day-to-day contact with their relatives.

STARTING OUT

Despite these troubles, the first wave of Vietnamese refugees settled into American life fairly easily. Their sponsors often helped their transition. Many also had advantages that helped them adapt to their new homeland:

1. The majority could speak English and knew at least a little about American ways.
2. About three-fourths had lived in urban areas in Vietnam, so they were familiar with modern city life.
3. A sizable percentage were Catholics. They could easily join churches, which provided them with an additional support system.
4. In comparison with most of the Vietnamese population, the refugees of 1975 were extremely well educated. About 48 percent of all heads of households had gone to high school. About 28 percent had attended college. (In Vietnam as a whole, less than 16 percent had a high school education, and less than 3 percent had any college training.)

In most cases, the refugees' education did not fully prepare them for the American workforce, and most refugees were so eager to set up their own households that they took whatever job they could find. They became maids, cooks, and factory laborers, working jobs that required little training and only the barest proficiency in English. Amazingly, by 1977, just two years after the refugees first arrived, 95 percent of

Vietnamese-American men and 93 percent of Vietnamese-American women were employed.

The 1975 refugees were strongly focused on making the most of their new lives in America. At the same time, Vietnam was never far from their minds. At quiet moments, the refugees could not help but wonder and worry about what was happening to the friends and relatives they left behind.

• Study Questions •

1. Why did many Vietnamese want to leave the country after North Vietnam won the war?

2. What types of dangers did Vietnamese refugees face when they fled?

3. How did the U.S. government prepare for the refugees' arrival?

4. How did most people get out of the American refugee camps?

5. What were the responsibilities of refugee sponsors?

6. What characteristics helped the 1975 Vietnamese refugees adapt quickly to American life?

4

The Boat People and Later Immigrants

When North Vietnam won the Vietnam War, many Vietnamese, even those who had not supported the Communists, hoped for the best. Pham, who grew up in Saigon, remembered, "The communists told us that they would treat us well. I thought that they would do as they said."[26] Regrettably, he was soon proved wrong:

> I was placed in a job working hard but the communists did not pay me enough to live. They kept telling us that we were traitors and that we had betrayed the real Vietnamese people. . . . Maybe we would earn the right to be Vietnamese again some day, but now we were just dogs."[27]

REEDUCATION

After the fall of Saigon, the first people to suffer at the hands of the Communists were the former soldiers and officials of the

Nghiem Vu, who spent 13 years in a Communist reeducation camp, views a display during a preview for the Oakland Museum of California's exhibit "What's Going on: California and the Vietnam Era," in August 2004. Prisoners such as Vu were often starved, beaten, and forced to perform hard labor at the camps, which were designed to indoctrinate the South Vietnamese in Communist ideology.

South Vietnamese government. Within a few weeks, the Communist government ordered several hundred thousand people to report to what were called *reeducation camps.* Supposedly, these people were to undergo intensive training in Communist *ideology.* In fact, the camps were prisons, where the inmates were starved, beaten, and forced to perform hard labor. An Thu described his ordeal in this way:

> After clearing trees and constructing the reeducation camp
> to which I have been sent, I was forced to clear the fields
> and remove the mines, which occasionally exploded and
> killed us prisoners. Then I planted corn and vegetables,

very hard work for me because I was in my forties and living on starvation rations.[28]

Some prisoners were held for just a few months, but others were in the camps for as long as 15 years. Many people died from illness or starvation. To survive, hungry prisoners ate anything they could find, including mice and crickets. Hung, a former army captain, recalled that inmates often died after an injured arm or leg was amputated: "The amputation of limbs was done with a handsaw, without anesthesia. . . . Everyone in the camp heard their terrible screams. Then their stumps became infected and they died."[29]

SURVIVING THE CAMPS

Prisoners suffered from mental as well as physical abuse. Their captors frequently interrogated them, demanding that they confess to imaginary crimes against the state. A businessman named Trinh was held in a reeducation camp for two years. He was told he would be released only if he confessed. He did four times, but his captors did not think he was sincere. He tried again: "I spoke for two hours denouncing America, my fellow traitors in Vietnam, and begging forgiveness for my awful crimes. I did not believe one thing that I said, but I learned that I can be a good actor if it is [that], or die."[30] His performance finally earned his freedom. After Trinh was let go, he went home to Saigon, only to find that the government had taken over his business.

Many survivors of the camps discovered their lives were changed forever. Some were left physically broken by the experience. Others saw their marriages crumble because of their long absence from their family. Still others were hounded by the authorities long after they were let go.

A REPRESSIVE GOVERNMENT

The reeducation camp inmates were the greatest victims of the new regime, but nearly everyone was affected by Vietnam's new repressive economic policies. Many people lost their livelihoods as the Communists began seizing private businesses. Others watched their savings become worthless, when the government repeatedly abolished the national currency. The government also disrupted the lives of millions of people in urban centers by forcing them to move to rural areas. There, these city people were made to work on government-run farms.

Adding to the country's financial troubles was a series of expensive conflicts Vietnam fought with China and Cambodia. By the late 1970s, Vietnam was plagued with high unemployment rates, food shortages, malnutrition, and increasing levels of poverty.

The Vietnamese also came to resent the government's intrusion on their private lives. Government agents were everywhere, ready to report and punish anyone who criticized the government. People were forced to spy on their friends, neighbors, and even their own family members. A Buddhist nun described the situation: "Parents dared not talk to their own children, for the next day the children might involuntarily reveal something to their friends at school. Even husbands and wives became wary of one another."[31]

DECIDING TO FLEE

The government's repressive policies left many Vietnamese angry and desperate. Even some people who had supported the Communists were horrified by the government's abuses. Many Vietnamese were so unhappy that they made the difficult decision to leave their homeland.

Even harder was figuring out how to do it. The Vietnamese were not allowed to leave the country without the government's permission. To get out, they had to escape, risking imprisonment if they were caught. In the first three years of Communist rule, only a few thousand people escaped, but by 1978, living conditions in Vietnam had become so bad that tens of thousands were desperate to flee.

Some bribed government officials to get help. Others fled over land through Cambodia. Most, however, just found a boat and headed out to sea, praying someone would rescue them. These refugees became known in the United States as *boat people*.

A boat person named Phuong Hoang spent a full year plotting his escape. He and a friend bought a boat and trained themselves in sea navigation. Even with all their planning, the escape nearly turned into a tragedy, when their boat began to sink. They would have died if an Italian ship had not come upon them by chance. Hoang later recalled his almost fatal adventure: "Looking back on it now, our sea voyage, with only a toy compass to guide us, was very dangerous. Still, it would have been better to die at sea than live another day under Communist rule."[32]

DANGEROUS ESCAPES

Not all boat people were so lucky. Many were caught by the authorities and forced to return to Vietnam. Nevertheless, some remained determined to escape. Some people tried two, three, four, or more times before finally making their way out of the country.

Those traveling by sea faced many dangers. The waters of the South China Sea are rough. Many boats, especially rickety homemade vessels, were lost during fearsome storms. Others were overtaken by Vietnamese soldiers patrolling the sea or pirates looking to steal their precious provisions. Most boats were small, so they had little room for food and water. Sometimes, boats drifted for weeks as the passengers died from starvation and dehydration.

The Vietnamese government did not keep a record of how many escapees died, but thousands did not survive the trip. Some scholars estimate that about 10 percent met their death at sea. Others believe as many as half the boat people died.

By the late 1970s, conditions in Vietnam had become so bad that tens of thousands of people began fleeing the country. Many who left Vietnam by sea were known as "boat people," including this group of refugees in the South China Sea, near Saigon.

REFUGEE CAMPS

If boat people were rescued or made it to shore, they were usually taken to a refugee camp. Several countries—including Thailand, Malaysia, Indonesia, Singapore, and the Philippines—set up camps to deal with the escaping Vietnamese. These camps filled up quickly as more and more Vietnamese fled. One camp, located off Malaysia on the small, uninhabited island of Pulau Bidong, eventually housed 42,000 Vietnamese on slightly more than one-half square mile (1.3 square kilometers) of land.

The conditions at these overcrowded camps were horrible. Already exhausted by their terrifying sea journey, refugees lived in hastily built shelters with little food and water. The worst camps were like prisons, policed by brutal guards. One young person remembered being tortured at a Thai camp: "For minor infractions, the guards would string us up by our thumbs and leave us hanging until we passed out. To make sure we were unconscious, they would burn us with lighted cigarettes."[33]

For some, the worst part of camp life was not knowing when they would be able to leave or where they might be sent. A man named Van explained his anguish, as he whiled away day after day, with nothing to do but worry: "The hours of waiting were the worst. I missed my country and I could only imagine what the communists were doing to our friends and neighbors. I tried to find out about friends of ours, but no one had any information."[34]

THE REFUGEE ACT

The world was horrified by the death and suffering of the Vietnamese boat people. The United Nations (UN), an international organization founded to promote peace among nations, realized the need for a plan to make their flight easier and safer. It also saw that more countries had to be persuaded to take in the refugees, because few Asian nations were willing to accept large numbers of Vietnamese as permanent residents.

First-Person Account

"BOAT PERSON" ANTON VO

After three failed attempts, Anton Vo finally escaped Vietnam in a boat with 41 other passengers. He made his way to Buffalo, New York, where he learned English and obtained a degree from the University of Buffalo. Vo eventually became a high school teacher in Memphis, Tennessee. His story of how he came to America was published in *Voices of Vietnamese Boat People* in 2000:

We spent two weeks on the sea in an open boat. The first two days we were seasick, but after that we could stand up and look at the sky and the water. That was all you could see, just water and sky. . . .

After one week we ran out of water and out of food. So we fished and ate the fish raw. After ten days, the engine stopped working. . . .

During our two weeks on the sea, two people died because they drank seawater. . . . After they died, we threw them into the sea.

After we got to the land, we just lay down and slept. We were like dead bodies on the seashore. . . . [T]hen we went to the refugee camp.

Within a month, government officials from lots of countries . . . had interviewed us for immigration. . . . Then one day in school I heard my number on the public-address system. They said those called were to go home and get dressed and prepare to go to Bataan, Philippines. We were to transfer to Bataan and later be transferred to America. Oh man! I was so happy.*

* Mary Terrell Cargill and Jade Quang Huynh, eds., *Voices of the Vietnamese Boat People: Nineteen Narratives of Escape and Survival* (Jefferson, N.C.: McFarland, 2000), 114–117.

To address these problems, the UN developed the Orderly Departure Program (ODP) in 1979. It convinced 20 countries, including the United States and Canada, to allow refugees to resettle within their borders.

To implement the ODP, the U.S. Congress passed the Refugee Act of 1980. It allowed Vietnamese refugees to come directly to America, bypassing the refugee camps, if they had specific ties to the United States. For instance, refugees with a close relative in America or with a history of employment with a U.S. company were welcome.

The Refugee Act certainly made it easier for Vietnamese refugees to enter the United States, but this was neither a quick nor a simple process. Under the ODP, the U.S. government had to agree to accept a refugee and the Vietnamese government had to agree to let him go. Would-be refugees found that just applying to leave Vietnam could put them in jeopardy. Vietnam authorities often harassed applicants, barring them from holding a job or going to school. Some officials held up applications until they received a substantial bribe.

EXPELLING THE UNWANTED

In determining who could leave and who had to stay, the Vietnamese government was generally uninterested in whether the applicant met the conditions of the ODP. Instead, it used the program to get rid of people it considered undesirable. These included ethnic Chinese and *Amerasians.*

The ethnic Chinese were people of Chinese ancestry living in Vietnam. For some 400 years, the ethnic Chinese had been an important minority in the country. They were active in business in the nation's urban centers. After the Communist takeover, the government confiscated their wealth and businesses. The ethnic Chinese also suffered increased discrimination as Vietnam's clashes with China stirred up anti-Chinese sentiment.

Vietnamese Immigrants Admitted Under Different Preference Categories, 1998 to 2004

Year	Total	Family-sponsored preferences	Employment-based preferences	Immediate relatives of U.S. citizens (Total)	Spouses of U.S. citizens	Children	Parents
2004	31,514	14,890	D*	10,338	7,527	1,176	1,635
2003	22,133	11,124	119	9,099	6,245	1,377	1,477
2002	33,627	12,810	297	12,984	8,472	2,174	2,338
2001	35,531	11,841	273	12,271	7,720	1,964	2,587
2000	26,747	10,473	148	9,121	5,585	1,653	1,883
1999	20,393	8,883	74	6,311	3,592	1,355	1,364
1998	17,649	6,857	96	5,139	2,778	1,134	1,227

Source: Department of Homeland Security Web site. Available online at *http://www.uscis.gov/graphics/shared/statistics/yearbook/2004/table2.xls*

*Disclosure standard not met.

The Amerasians were the children of Vietnamese women and U.S. soldiers. After the pullout of U.S. troops from Vietnam, the Amerasians were considered outcasts in Vietnamese society. They were often mistreated because of their American ancestry. Some were abandoned by their mothers, forcing them to make their way alone as street children.

U.S. officials felt a moral obligation to help these children. Initially, they were allowed to come to the United States only if they had sponsors, but it was often difficult to find sponsors for Amerasians. Many were scorned by their Vietnamese-American relatives, and most did not even know who their American parent was. To ease the Amerasians' immigration to the United States, the U.S. Congress passed the Amerasian Homecoming Act in December 1987, which helped Amerasians and their immediate families enter the country. In some cases, however, Vietnamese families adopted Amerasian children so they could enter the United States, only to abandon the children once they arrived.

The United States also made special arrangements for released refugee camp prisoners. The Vietnamese government often held up applications of people they considered political enemies. Vietnamese officials feared the former prisoners might try to plot an overthrow of the Vietnamese government while living abroad. In 1988, the U.S. State Department finally negotiated with Vietnam for the resettlement of tens of thousands of former prisoners through its humanitarian operation. Prisoners had to have been in the camps for at least three years to qualify.

THE COMPREHENSIVE PLAN OF ACTION

Despite these efforts, the United States was far from solving the problems associated with the mass emigration of Vietnamese. Vietnamese continued to flee to the camps in Southeast Asia, but as the Asian nations grew more and more reluctant to admit them as citizens, the camps became increasingly crowded. To deal with the situation, the United States convened an international conference in Geneva, Switzerland, in 1989.

Seventy-eight participating countries signed the Comprehensive Plan of Action (CPA). Under this plan, the camp inmates would be screened to see if they were refugees—that is, people who experienced or rightly feared persecution by their government. Refugees would be resettled in other nations. Those who did not meet this criteria, however, would be returned to Vietnam. The CPA, therefore, made it more difficult for people to leave Vietnam just to escape the economic troubles there.

Screeners found that only about 20 percent of the camp inmates were true refugees. In 1996, the last of the Asian refugee camps was closed, after many Vietnamese escapees had been forced to return to Vietnam against their will. (Approximately 18,000 returnees were eventually resettled in the United States under the 1996 Resettlement Opportunity for Vietnamese Returnees Program, however.) Although a personal disaster for the returned refugees, the CPA achieved its political ends: The number of Vietnamese willing to make dangerous escapes by sea dropped dramatically, ending the humanitarian crisis associated with the boat people.

• Study Questions •

1. What happened in Vietnam's reeducation camps?

2. What did the Vietnamese government do that made many people want to flee the country?

3. Who were the boat people?

4. What were the goals of the Orderly Departure Program?

5. Who were the Amerasians?

6. What was the Comprehensive Plan of Action?

5

Settling In

According to the U.S. census, in the year 2000 there were about 1,122,528 people of Vietnamese ancestry living in the United States. (In the same year, an additional 151,000 lived in Canada.) Twenty-five years after the end of the Vietnam War, Vietnamese Americans made up about 0.4 percent of the total population and about 11 percent of all Asian Americans.

About one-quarter of Vietnamese Americans were born in the United States. Of those who were foreign born, nearly half arrived fairly recently. About 49 percent came after 1990, about 31 percent between 1980 and 1989, and about 20 percent before 1980. The period in which these immigrants arrived had a significant impact on their adaptation to American life. On a basic level, however, all faced the same challenge: finding a way to fit in, in a new land, with unfamiliar institutions and customs.

BECOMING SELF SUFFICIENT

For most recent arrivals, finding employment was the highest priority. The first wave of Vietnamese Americans were especially eager to find work. Only by becoming financially independent could they leave their sponsors and set up their own households. For many, a paycheck also meant they could send money to relatives still in Vietnam. Another incentive to find work was the Vietnamese work ethic. In Vietnamese culture, unemployment was considered shameful, especially among men. Men risked losing status among their friends and family if they did not hold down a job.

Many Vietnamese immigrants were also not comfortable receiving financial help from the U.S. government. The Indochina Migration and Refugee Assistance Act of 1975 allowed for three years of assistance to help these refugees resettle in the United States. (This was reduced to 18 months in 1982, then to 8 months in 1992.) Many Vietnamese Americans, however, preferred earning an income to receiving a government check, even though this often caused their families financial hardship. As one Vietnamese immigrant in Oklahoma explained,

> I am thankful to the government for their help, but I do not need it [anymore]. I think that a person should support their family as soon they can and not ask for outside help. My new country has been good to me, and I want to show my appreciation by helping myself and helping others as soon as I can.[35]

FINDING A JOB

Despite their determination, finding a good job was not always easy, even for the first-wave immigrants, many of whom were well educated. People who had worked in medicine, law, and other professions discovered that, despite their training and experience, they could not resume their careers without further education in America. One Vietnamese-American physician in Oklahoma bitterly explained his frustration:

In Saigon, I was a surgeon and had practiced for many years. When I come here, I am told that I must be a beginner again and serve like an apprentice for two years. I have no choice so I will do it, but I have been wronged to be asked to do this. I am a good doctor and I do not have to be treated like a second-class [physician].[36]

The United States offered the earliest Vietnamese immigrants free job training for three years. The training, however, was mostly for low-paying, entry-level positions, such as factory work. At least at first, most new arrivals looked for work that required no skills. People who were professors, doctors, politicians, or soldiers in Vietnam became day laborers, janitors, dishwashers, or night security guards. Often, they had to work odd hours or take unstable, part-time jobs. One man in Houston described his struggles with employment: "I have a job at a little store where I work from 10 at night to 8 o'clock in the morning. I do not like to leave my family at night, but it is the only job I can find. I am looking and I will find another job soon so I can work in the day."[37]

Not all Vietnamese Americans suffered a loss in employment status. Some immigrants, especially those among the later waves, which arrived in the 1980s, had been poor in their home country. Many were rural people who had had to work extremely hard just to eke out a living. For these immigrants, the chance to work in a factory, for instance, was a step up, since the work paid a living wage and did not involve hard labor.

As time passed, many Vietnamese Americans were able to find better jobs. Some went to school to train for new professions. Others started their own businesses. When the first immigrants arrived, starting a business was difficult because, with no credit history, Vietnamese Americans had trouble persuading banks to grant them business loans. Generally, they instead had to borrow money from other Vietnamese, most of whom had little cash to invest.

Even so, many *entrepreneurs* were able to slowly build successful businesses. For instance, one man who had been a government official in Vietnam started a lawn-care business in Hawaii that eventually employed nine crews of workers. He described his pride in his achievements: "I teach my boys that it is important to work for your living and that all hard work is honorable. I have changed from being a Vietnamese government official to being an American businessman. I am proud of what I do and of how my family has become Americans."[38]

According to the 2000 U.S. census, Vietnamese Americans are now employed in a variety of jobs. About 30 percent work in professions or management, about 27 percent in production and transportation, about 19 percent in service, about 19 percent in sales and office work, and about 6 percent in construction and maintenance.

Although their employment prospects have improved over time, about 16 percent of Vietnamese Americans live in poverty. (The rate is about 12 percent for all Americans.) In addition, Vietnamese-American workers make somewhat less than the national average. Among all American workers, the average income is $37,057 for men and $27,194 for women. Among Vietnamese Americans, the average income is $31,258 for men and $24,028 for women. The gap in household income is less substantial ($50,046 for all families versus $47,103 for Vietnamese-American ones), probably because Vietnamese-American households tend to include more adults of working age. About 68 percent of Vietnamese-American men and about 56 percent of Vietnamese-American women are employed.

HOUSING NEEDS

For most Vietnamese families, the first priority after becoming financially stable was finding a home of their own. Many had trouble locating adequate housing. With no assets, it was hard to get a mortgage to buy a house. Most had no choice but to rent an apartment. Some landlords were hesitant to rent

Notable Individual
ACTRESS KIEU CHINH

Kieu Chinh survived war and hardship to become an internationally renowned actress. The daughter of an official of the French government in Vietnam, she was born in 1937 in Hanoi. When the French were driven out, Chinh and her family tried to flee North Vietnam.

Only Chinh was able to escape. She settled in Saigon, where she began her acting career. By the late 1960s, she was a famous film star throughout Southeast Asia. Chinh also appeared in several American films, including *A Yank in Vietnam* (1964) and *Operation C.I.A.* (1965).

With the fall of Saigon, Chinh was forced once again to flee her home. She reached Toronto, Canada, where she took menial jobs, just to get by. Chinh, however, was determined to revive her film career. With help from American actress Tippi Hedren, she moved to Los Angeles, California, and began looking for work. She soon began landing roles in television (most notably on the series *M*A*S*H*) and in movies, such as *The Joy Luck Club* (1993), *Green Dragon* (2001), and *Journey from the Fall* (2005). Chinh also received an Emmy Award for her documentary *Kieu Chinh: A Journey Home* (1996).

Chinh is a cofounder of the Vietnam Children's Fund (VCF). With Vietnam veteran Lewis B. Puller, Jr., and journalist Terry Anderson, she established this charity to create a "living memorial" to the Vietnamese people killed in war. Using funds collected throughout the world, the Vietnam Children's Fund is building a network of new schools in Vietnam, which will eventually provide classroom space for 58,000 children. Through her charitable work, Chinh hopes to help both Vietnamese and Americans heal the wounds of the Vietnam War: "I think the most important thing we can do is understand each other. We can forgive and forget. We can care and love each other."*

* John Gittelsohn, "The Struggle to Forgive," the *Orange County Register*. Available online at *www.vietnamchildren.org/kieu/chapter11.shtml*.

to Vietnamese immigrants, either because of prejudice or because Vietnamese-American households tended to be large.

For recent immigrants, there were many advantages to living in large households. Financially, all the adults could pool their income and government checks and share expenses. Emotionally, they could help one another during difficult times. In terms of finding housing, having large households worked against the immigrants. With low incomes, families generally could only afford to rent small apartments, but the fire codes of many communities limited the number of people who could live in small dwellings. One man in San Antonio described his family's difficulties in finding a place to live: "We had a hard time finding a house to live in. Because there were 11 of us nobody wanted to rent us a place. They showed us places which were big but we could not afford them."[39]

Today, Vietnamese Americans still tend to live in larger households (average size, 3.7 persons) than Americans as a whole (average size, 2.6 persons). But they have become more prosperous; more and more Vietnamese-American families have been able to buy homes of their own. Now, about 53 percent have achieved home ownership. This for many Vietnamese Americans is a particularly important symbol of success.

LEARNING THE LANGUAGE

For Vietnamese immigrants, learning English was just as important as finding a job and a home. This was easiest for the immigrants who left Vietnam directly after the war. Most had some knowledge of English, and some, particularly those who had worked for Americans, were fairly fluent. They could translate for family and friends who had little or no command of English.

The situation was different for the boat people and other later immigrants. Most did not know English, and because English and Vietnamese are very different, they found the language difficult to learn. It was particularly hard for rural people who had never received an education in Vietnam. As one

Upon entering the United States, the first priority for many Vietnamese immigrants was learning English. Pictured here are Vietnamese-American children being taught the English words for nose, eye, and mouth at Fort Chaffee, in Arkansas.

Vietnamese immigrant explained: "When I got to America, I did not read my own language [Vietnamese] so good, but I was a farmer. In this place, I have to read to eat. That makes it hard for me but it makes me force [myself] to learn."[40]

Even after 30 years of immigration, few Vietnamese Americans—only about 7 percent—speak only English at home. Of those who speak primarily Vietnamese at home, only 31 percent feel they have the ability to speak English "very well."

AMERICAN WAYS

Just as knowledge of English eased the way for many Vietnamese Americans, so did an understanding of American customs.

Even people who were friendly with Americans in Vietnam were sometimes baffled or put off by American behavior.

Traditionally, Vietnamese valued harmony and humility. The competitive spirit praised in American society made many Vietnamese Americans uncomfortable. One Vietnamese-American man described his preference for cooperation over competition: "I should never think of myself first or better [than anyone else]. That is hard for my American friends who think that winning is being better. Being better is working together so that everybody wins. Nobody wins alone. No one [alone] should take credit for victory."[41]

Another man, from Dallas, Texas, recounted an incident in which he inadvertently angered his sponsor: "My sponsor asked me to go to his church, but I cannot go [because] I am a Buddhist. I could not also say 'no' because I do not want to be ungrateful for all his help. So I say 'yes' to make him feel good and know that I like him. When I did not go, he called and was upset, but he did not say why."[42] For this Vietnamese man, appearing ungrateful would be a much greater wrong than not keeping his promise, especially since, in his eyes, the sponsor's request had been completely inappropriate in the first place.

BUILDING COMMUNITIES

Understandably, many Vietnamese immigrants were most comfortable in the company of one another. Because of the U.S. government's dispersal policy, the first wave of immigrants were sent to locations all across the country, making it difficult for Vietnamese Americans to form their own communities.

After becoming financially self sufficient, however, many immigrants were no longer happy in the areas where they were resettled. Some lived in small towns where they did not feel fully accepted by their neighbors. Others lived in northern regions and disliked the winter weather there. Many just wanted to move to a place where they could be near friends, relatives, or merely other immigrants who shared their culture and language.

Approximately 40 percent of Vietnamese Americans live in California, and many communities within the state have sections known as "Little Saigons," where these immigrants have settled. Pictured here is a store in Orange County's Westminster community, which is the nation's oldest and largest Little Saigon.

Consequently, by 1980, about two-thirds of the Vietnamese-American population had concentrated in just seven states—California, Texas, Louisiana, Virginia, Washington, Pennsylvania, and Florida. In 2000, California alone was the home of about 40 percent of all Vietnamese Americans. Today, many live in Orange and Los Angeles counties. Orange County towns, including Garden Grove, Santa Ana, Anaheim, and Westminster, have particularly large Vietnamese-American populations.

States with the Highest Population of Vietnamese Americans, 2000	
State	**Vietnamese-American Population**
California	444,032
Texas	134,961
Washington	46,149
Virginia	37,309
Massachusetts	33,962

HELPING HANDS

These communities have become a vital part of the lives of Vietnamese Americans. The neighborhoods are home to many businesses—including food shops, restaurants, and newspapers—for Vietnamese Americans run by Vietnamese Americans. They also provide a source of comfort and support, most importantly for immigrants who have recently arrived in the United States.

In 1975, when the first mass migration occurred, there were relatively few Vietnamese living in America. As a result, these early immigrants had to rely mostly on the government for financial aid and help in adjusting to their new land. As these Vietnamese Americans prospered and developed their communities, they began creating their own organizations to help those who arrived later.

In many areas, new immigrants can now seek out *mutual assistance associations* (MAAs). These organizations, run by Vietnamese Americans, offer a variety of services. Probably most important are language classes. One man in Southern California explained the significant role such classes played in his life:

> When I came to America I did not speak any English and I did not understand. I could not read the signs, and I could not fill out the forms. My [Vietnamese] friends in the community told me of the classes and I attend. They have helped me to make a

good life here and last week I passed my first English test. One day before [too] long, I will take the test and be a citizen.[43]

MAAs also offer instruction in all sorts of practical matters, including how to find a job, how to drive a car, and how to read a contract. From their own experiences, settled Vietnamese Americans can best understand what aspects of American society are especially confusing for new arrivals. Some organizations, for instance, offer classes in how to shop in an American grocery store. Not only are many American meats, fruits, and vegetables unfamiliar to Vietnamese immigrants, but American packaged goods can also be baffling. In Oklahoma City, an MAA began escorting newcomers to the supermarket after one woman had a disturbing experience on her first shopping trip. Believing that pictures on goods represented their contents, the woman saw a baby on a jar of baby food and concluded Americans were cannibals. Able to anticipate difficulties that U.S. government agencies could not, the MAAs have been instrumental in helping many new immigrants survive and ultimately thrive.

• Study Questions •

1. How many Vietnamese Americans were living in the United States in the year 2000?

2. Why have some Vietnamese Americans had trouble finding housing?

3. Why did many Vietnamese Americans move within a few years after arriving in the United States?

4. Which state has the highest Vietnamese-American population?

5. What is a mutual assistance association?

6

Making It in America

Within years of the arrival of the first wave of Vietnamese immigrants, the media began to hail their accomplishments. Major magazines called them a "super minority" and dubbed young Vietnamese-American students as "whiz kids." (Other Asian-American groups have also been dubbed "model minorities.")

Although the press seemed much more interested in Vietnamese immigrants' successes than their struggles, there was some truth to the glowing accounts. Many Vietnamese Americans, especially some of the earliest immigrants, quickly made enormous strides. Particularly noteworthy were their achievements as students and as entrepreneurs.

A LOVE OF LEARNING

The Vietnamese Americans' educational success was rooted in their home country's traditions. The Vietnamese talk of a quality called *tran hieu hoc*—roughly translated as "a love of learning." One popular folk story suggests its importance in Vietnamese life. The story tells of a young boy who started to build a kite from an old piece of rice paper. Watching him, his grandmother realized the paper was marked with writing. She snatched it from the boy's hands and set it on fire. In her eyes, the writing on the paper represented ideas and scholarship. These were so revered, that it was better to destroy the paper than turn it into a plaything. For the Vietnamese, education is a serious undertaking, with no room for fun and frivolity.

Their high esteem for education dated from the period when the Chinese ruled Vietnam. Under the Chinese, mandarins were high-ranking officials who helped run the government. In order to become a mandarin, a man had to pass an extremely difficult series of examinations. Passing the exams brought great honor not only to the student but also to his family and his village.

When the French controlled Vietnam, very few Vietnamese were allowed to attend school. After 1954, more schools opened up, especially in the south, but education still remained an impossible dream for many. With educational opportunities so rare and precious in their home country, many immigrants were understandably delighted that every child in America was able to attend public schools. Vietnamese-American parents were determined that their children would make the most of this opportunity.

THE WHIZ KIDS

Parental pressure to achieve was certainly one reason Vietnamese-American students performed so well. From an early age, children were told to make schooling their top priority. Many parents shared their own stories of working menial jobs for low pay, emphasizing how difficult life could be without a formal education.

Vietnamese-American students tended to excel in mathematics and science. Some focused on these subjects because they could be mastered with a limited command of English. In college, Vietnamese Americans often majored in computer science, engineering, and medicine, for the same reason. Also, these fields were chosen because they pay fairly well. Since young people were expected to contribute financially to the family, parents were apt to push children toward more financially lucrative professions, sometimes disregarding their children's own interests or talents.

Like the mandarins of the past, talented students reflected well on their families. On the other hand, within the Vietnamese community, students who performed poorly brought their parents shame. One parent explained the pressure these beliefs placed on his own children: "[M]y children know that if they become doctor or become engineer, I share it with them, and our friends and neighbors share it. But if they fail, we all fail."[44]

Considering educational achievement as a family project, many parents were very involved in their children's schooling. They asked about the children's lessons, discussed their grades, and made sure their homework was done. These parents were often suspicious of American popular culture. They feared that television, movies, and music were unnecessary distractions liable to disrupt their children's ability to succeed.

The students' reputation as "whiz kids" might also have contributed to their success. Teachers often expected more from them, and upholding their reputation contributed to their hard work.

TAKING CARE OF BUSINESS

Talented Vietnamese-American students were not the only ones who found themselves with lucrative jobs. Many other Vietnamese Americans, through determination and hard work, carved out successful careers. For many Vietnamese Americans, the difficult journey to the United States fueled their desire to do well. One woman named That Thao arrived in America in 1981, after making 10 attempts to escape. Surviving years of Communist rule, she described the United States as "like heaven." Waiting to make the most of the opportunities she found, That Thao worked two full-time jobs, while also attending school. As she explained, "In America I learn to manage my time and use it well. I used to be shy and insecure. Now I am very open and confident in myself. I believe I get better every day. Nothing can stop me; I can do what I want."[45]

Some Vietnamese Americans found that starting a business from the ground up was the shortest road to success. Often, these businesses were family owned and operated. Every member of the family, usually even children, pitched in, and together they shared in the profits. According to the National Congress of Vietnamese Americans, Vietnamese-American–owned businesses now employ about 97,000 people and generate annual receipts of more than $9 billion.

Vietnamese-American entrepreneurs had a particularly strong impact on two industries. One is the fishing and shrimping business along the Gulf Coast. In the late 1970s, Vietnamese-American fishermen began moving to Texas and Louisiana to practice their profession. At first, most took low-paying jobs, helping American fishermen and cleaning fish. In time, some of these immigrants pooled their resources and bought their own fishing boats. Although they often met opposition from their American competitors, Vietnamese Americans now make up a large percentage of shrimpers working in the Gulf of Mexico.

After growing prosperous in the 1990s, these shrimpers have recently faced challenges that threaten their livelihood. The importation of low-priced shrimp has cut into their profits. More devastatingly, in 2005, Hurricane Katrina destroyed many of these shrimpers' boats and homes, forcing some to start their lives over again.

Other Vietnamese Americans have found success in the nail-care industry. These entrepreneurs discovered that nail salons

CELEBRATING TET

Little Saigons are always lively, but these areas are especially exciting during the holiday of Tet, which is celebrated on the first day of the first month of the lunar calendar. (The exact date varies, falling sometime between January 19 and February 20.) Tet is considered the Vietnamese New Year, but as sociologist Hien Duc Do has pointed out, it means much more than that: "For the Vietnamese, it is the equivalent of Thanksgiving Day, Memorial Day, New Year's Day, and birthdays all combined into one massive celebration. As such, it symbolizes new beginnings and the rebirth of the Vietnamese culture."*

Vietnamese Americans often spend weeks preparing for Tet. They clean their houses, decorate them with flowers, and buy new clothes. The actual celebration takes place over several days. People spend time with their friends and family and burn offerings for their ancestors. Children are expected to extend good wishes to adults, who reward them with gifts of money in red envelopes. Everyone enjoys treats associated with Tet, including meat rolls, candied fruit, and perfumed tea.

By celebrating Tet, Vietnamese Americans restore their ties to one another and to their community. For older people, it is also a time to reminisce and share wonderful memories of the old country with younger people, who may never have celebrated Tet in Vietnam. As one adolescent explained, the holiday also helps young people define what it means to be a Vietnamese American:

I like the Tet celebration. It is a time when we can party and have a good time together. . . . I don't understand what it all means, but

require little money to start up and that the training time needed to become a nail technician is short. Fairly quickly, a family

*Tet is a way of just being Vietnamese. For my folks it is a way of
remembering. For me it is a way of saying that that's kind of a part
of me, but so is America.***

Tet, the Vietnamese New Year, is celebrated on the first day of the
first month of the lunar calendar. An important part of the festival is
the Lion Dance, which serves to ward off evil spirits and bring good
luck. Here, onlookers in downtown Oakland, California, watch a Lion
Dance performance during Tet.

---

* Paul James Rutledge, *The Vietnam Experience in America* (Bloomington: Indiana University Press, 1992), 136.
** Ibid., 137–138.

could acquire the necessary funds and education to establish a salon of its own. Largely because of Vietnamese Americans' embrace of the nail-care industry, it has grown quickly, making professional nail care affordable to middle-income Americans. Today, Vietnamese Americans make up about 37 percent of licensed nail-care technicians in the United States and about 80 percent in California.

LITTLE SAIGONS

Many of the earliest Vietnamese-owned businesses catered almost exclusively to Vietnamese Americans. Particularly popular were food shops or restaurants offering traditional Vietnamese fare. Such businesses required few start-up costs, and those that were needed were usually borrowed from Vietnamese Americans who had a little extra money to invest. The establishments also had a ready and easily reachable clientele—other Vietnamese Americans eager for a taste of Vietnamese foods that were hard to find in America. Over time, however, many Vietnamese restaurants began attracting non-Vietnamese diners. Today, just about every city in the United States boasts at least one Vietnamese restaurant.

In the late 1970s, when Vietnamese Americans began to concentrate in certain areas, these communities attracted a wide variety of Vietnamese-owned businesses, from clothing outlets to record stores to beauty shops. These establishments were often operated in mini-malls along a central street. The Vietnamese-American communities concentrated around these shopping districts were soon nicknamed "Little Saigons."

Perhaps the most famous Little Saigon is in Westminster, California. Vietnamese Americans from throughout Southern California flock to the shops on a mile-long stretch on Bolsa Avenue. There, visitors can buy books and videotapes in Vietnamese, shop for herbs and traditional medicines in Vietnamese pharmacies, eat in Vietnamese restaurants, and enjoy themselves in karaoke night clubs. Also in the area are offices of

Vietnamese-American doctors, lawyers, accountants, and dentists. These professionals have many clients whose proficiency in English is too limited for them to seek these services elsewhere. Westminster's Little Saigon is now home to more than 3,500 Vietnamese-American businesses.

For many Vietnamese Americans, especially recent arrivals, dealing with American society is continually stressful. To them, a visit to a Little Saigon is like a vacation from their everyday life. There, they can relax, speak their old language, and spend time with people with similar backgrounds. One successful Vietnamese-American business owner explained the allure of Westminster's Little Saigon: "[W]hen the weekend comes, I want to go to Little Saigon, see a little bit of Vietnamese culture, drink some coffee, eat some noodle soup, meet old friends, and listen to them 'yak yak yak.' Then I feel good and at ease again."[46]

• Study Questions •

1. Why were Vietnamese Americans called a "model minority"?

2. Name two reasons Vietnamese Americans valued education.

3. What were popular majors with Vietnamese-American college students?

4. What is a "Little Saigon"?

5. Where is the most famous Little Saigon?

7

Everyday Struggles

Soon after the first Vietnamese refugees arrived, the press hailed their economic and educational successes. Far less was said about the difficulties Vietnamese immigrants faced in coming to the United States. Many—especially the well-educated early refugees—quickly rose to the challenge of adjusting to American society, but many others did not. Especially among later immigrants, the pressures and struggles they coped with every day made it nearly impossible to build a happy and productive life.

FITTING IN

Many Vietnamese immigrants came to the United States with some understanding of American culture, either from earlier contact with Americans or from news shared by earlier immigrants. Even so, sometimes the most basic aspects of American life proved frustrating to new Vietnamese Americans. Many

Some Vietnamese immigrants had a difficult time acclimating to American culture. Others, such as this couple in Pittsburgh, Pennsylvania, adopted American clothing and even changed their first names.

disliked the American diet, particularly fast food. As one Vietnamese man in Denver, Colorado, explained, "My children like it but when I go in I can smell the grease and it makes me sick."[47]

Others had trouble getting around their communities. When many people arrived, they did not have enough money to buy a car, and even if mass transit was available in their area, the systems seemed too complicated and confusing for recent immigrants to master. An elderly woman in Fort Worth, Texas, spoke of her discomfort with that city's bus system: "If I took the wrong thing [bus] I could be lost and not get back. I am afraid of being lost in such a big place."[48]

For many immigrants, limited English skills made just about every day-to-day task difficult. Obviously, with little English it was hard to find a job or an apartment. It also made shopping for necessities, visiting a doctor, or going to a restaurant an ordeal. For later arrivals, these problems were lessened. To improve their English, they could enlist support from mutual assistance associations, or they could shop and conduct business in Little Saigon districts. However, later immigrants complained that Vietnamese Americans from the first wave were not always as helpful as they should have been. One young woman named Vi expressed this view: "People in America were not friendly, including the Vietnamese who had come earlier. They did not want to mix with the new arrivals. So I felt sad."[49]

Unfortunately, the new arrivals lagged behind the first-wave immigrants in one crucial way—many families continued to live in poverty. Getting on a firm financial footing was especially hard for former reeducation camp prisoners and people who spent years in foreign refugee camps waiting for resettlement. These hardships left many immigrants physically and psychologically unprepared for the American job force.

TROUBLE IN SCHOOL

Despite their reputation as gifted students, the American school system was a source of anxiety for many Vietnamese young people. Some had trouble adjusting to the expectations of students in American classrooms. In the United States, children were supposed to look at the teacher and speak up in class. In Vietnam, students were expected *not* to make eye contact with their instructors, as a sign of respect. In addition, because of their deep reverence for education, they were never to question or talk back to their teachers. One boy in the eleventh grade at a Dallas, Texas, high school explained his difficult adjustment: "It took me a long time to learn that I am supposed to talk back [question] my teacher. My father got very angry with me for doing this, but I will not do well in school if I sit passively and do not ask questions."[50] All too often, American teachers were unaware of these differences in cultural norms. They tended to misinterpret Vietnamese Americans' humility and just assume the students were not paying attention.

For other Vietnamese-American students, the entire school environment was unfamiliar. Some, especially those from rural areas, never had the chance to go to school in their home country. Others spent many years in foreign refugee camps, where their education was virtually ignored. Once in America, these young people were often placed in grades according to their age, dealing with subjects too advanced for them to grasp. Unsurprisingly, some felt lost in the classroom. Vietnamese-American student Vi explained her miserable experience with American-style education:

> When I came to America, I was placed in the eighth grade, even though I had missed three years of school and had completed only the fourth grade in Vietnam. I felt old and stupid. I didn't know anything or understand what the teachers said. I tried really hard, but it did no good. I

couldn't speak; I couldn't communicate. . . . I felt so bad, because a person cannot live without communication. I wanted to go back to [my refugee camp in] Hong Kong, even though there was no hope or future there.[51]

Vietnamese-American parents were very supportive of their children's schooling, but many had to work long hours to make ends meet. They were often away from home and largely unaware of their children's struggles, especially because their children were often too ashamed to mention them.

Taunts from other students also made school agonizing for some Vietnamese Americans. One ninth-grade girl described the anti-Asian name-calling she endured: "I was called 'fish breath' and it made me angry. I am not a 'chink' or a 'slant eye.' I do not like being called names and I know that most of my friends at school do not like it either."[52]

Fearing their American classmates, Vietnamese-American students often sought support from one another. They were not always sympathetic to one another's troubles, however. More established students sometimes made fun of new arrivals, calling them FOB ("fresh off the boat"). At the same time, students who seemed too eager to make friends with white Americans and adopt their ways were derided as Bananas (that is, yellow on the outside and white on the inside).

MENTAL ILLNESS

Vietnamese Americans frequently shared with one another their stories of how they came to the United States. Talking about these painful memories often created a bond between them. For some, talking about the past helped them get beyond it. For others, however, the trauma they endured was too great for them to recover from. During the war or after, they may have witnessed violence, endured torture or starvation, or suffered the deaths of parents, children, and friends.

Adding to their stress was their concern for loved ones still in Vietnam. Often, years passed before refugees heard any news about friends and relatives, and frequently, when they did receive news, it was not good. Learning that loved ones were dead, trapped in reeducation camps, or living in poverty only increased refugees' anxieties. One man described the misery behind the constant façade he presented to the world: "On the outside, I am like an American. I drive to work in my car. I eat hamburgers at lunch. But on the inside, I am Vietnamese; I cannot forget my mother, hungry in Vietnam while I have it easy here."[53]

Not surprisingly, these difficult experiences often resulted in depression and other mental disorders, but many Vietnamese Americans suffering from mental illness did not receive treatment. In resettling refugees, the United States did little to provide them with needed therapy, preferring instead to focus on making Vietnamese Americans economically stable.

An even greater obstacle to treatment, however, was the traditional Vietnamese taboo on mental problems. People feared being shunned if they admitted to mental illness or sought treatment. One woman explained her willingness to suffer in silence rather than risk being branded as crazy: "I have bad dreams and wake up crying but I cannot tell anyone. I feel guilty that I lived when some of my family died, but I just try to be quiet and go on. No one wants to hear me complain. That would not be good."[54]

DISAPPOINTMENT AND ANGER

Unrealistic expectations about the United States left some immigrants severely disappointed. In Vietnam, they heard America heralded as a land of opportunity. After they arrived, however, they found fewer opportunities than they had hoped.

At 24, one young man complained about the hopelessness he felt about ever getting ahead: "Before I left Vietnam, I thought it would be easy to work and make more money in the United States. But when I came here, I found it was very difficult because of my language difficulties. I cannot speak English so I cannot do anything."[55] He also noted the difference between Vietnamese and American culture:

> In Vietnam we lacked material things but felt at ease; in America, we have material things, but emotionally we don't feel at ease. Here we have responsibility, we must go to work on time; when I return home, I eat and worry about going back to sleep for the next day. Life is just like a circle here. We just go round and round.[56]

Some Vietnamese Americans already had misgivings about the United States before they arrived. Although they were grateful the country took them in as refugees, they often could not forget or forgive the U.S. military withdrawal during the Vietnam War. A man named Hung, who had served in the South Vietnamese Army and was later sent to a reeducation camp, recounted his bitter feelings: "A lot of Vietnamese believed that we lost because the Americans withdrew their military aid in 1973. . . . I figured that we had been betrayed and abandoned."[57]

These emotions are so overpowering for a few Vietnamese Americans that they are unable to get on with their lives. Sociologist Hien Duc Do has discussed a "Vietnam syndrome," in which immigrants, especially former military men, devote all their time and energy into denouncing Vietnam's Communist government. Obsessed with overthrowing the Communists in their homeland, they have difficulty concentrating on finding a place for themselves in America.

RACISM AND VIOLENCE

Vietnamese Americans were forced to deal with another disappointing element of American life—racism. Refugees in the first wave, in the mid-1970s, were often amazed at the warmth of their sponsors and others who reached out to help them. On the other hand, they also encountered substantial hostility from the American public.

At the time, the U.S. economy was in the doldrums, with unemployment and inflation running high. Some Americans took out their frustration on the Vietnamese flooding into the United States. They claimed the newcomers were a further drain on the economy, because they were receiving financial support from the government. (Congress arranged for the Vietnamese refugees to receive modest payments, but these were dramatically cut over time.) A few Americans said the government was providing the Vietnamese with free loans for houses and cars. There was no truth to this rumor. Some immigrants were able to make such purchases, but only after many relatives came together and pooled their income.

As time passed, Vietnamese Americans continued to be targets of resentment. Some were convinced the immigrants were taking jobs that rightfully belonged to native-born Americans. Particularly angry were white fishermen who worked along the coast of the Gulf of Mexico. After Vietnamese fishermen came to the area, the whites claimed that the Vietnamese were competing with them unfairly. They were justified in their complaints that, by catching undersized fish and using oversized nets, the Vietnamese were not following the law. The main reason many Vietnamese were more successful at fishing, though, was that they were willing to work longer and harder.

In 1979, in Seadrift, Texas, the hostility toward Vietnamese fishermen turned violent. There, two Vietnamese Americans killed a white fisherman who had been harassing them. A jury ruled that the Vietnamese Americans acted in self-defense. The townspeople, however, were not satisfied. They began threatening the refugees living there. Several of their homes and boats were set on fire. About two-thirds of the 130 Vietnamese living in Seadrift fled in terror.

Non-Christian Vietnamese Americans also encountered hostility because of their religion. In one instance, residents of Oklahoma City began shouting racist remarks and threatened Vietnamese neighbors after they constructed a Buddhist temple. One angry Oklahoman was quoted as saying: "We don't need these chinks around here screwing up our kids. There are places where they can go but it ain't here. If I wanted some un-American fish-eater in my neighborhood, I'd go kill [him] . . . and plant him in the backyard."[58]

Sadly, Vietnamese Americans were also targeted by people of other minority groups. These groups were often convinced the government was showing preferential treatment to the newly arrived Vietnamese. For example, in 1979, Hispanic Americans began to vandalize the cars and homes of Vietnamese-American residents of Lincoln Park, a Denver, Colorado, housing project. The vandals believed that the Vietnamese were taking over the project, which traditionally had Hispanic residents. One Vietnamese-American woman mournfully described the violence: "I lived in the apartment when some of the boys came and broke our windows. I was afraid that they would hurt me and I was also afraid my husband might hurt someone because he was so angry. I did not want to see anyone hurt, and I did not want my husband to go to jail."[59]

One of the most tragic incidents of violence against Vietnamese Americans occurred in Stockton, California, in 1989. At the Cleveland Elementary School, a man fired an assault rifle into the playground. He was specifically trying to kill Asian-American children. One of the five children killed was a Vietnamese American.

GANGS

Vietnamese Americans were also threatened by members of their own community. Young Vietnamese-American men in their teens and early 20s began to form gangs. Like most gang members, they were often poor and hopeless, with few expectations for the future. Alienated from their surroundings and estranged from their relatives, they frequently looked to gangs for the companionship and comfort otherwise missing from their lives.

Vietnamese-American gangs often went by names that referred to their ethnicity—for example, Asian Boys, A.W.A (meaning "Asians with attitude"), and B.T.K. (meaning "born to kill," a slogan some American soldiers painted on their helmets during the Vietnam War). To show their gang affiliation, gang members often got tattoos of tigers, dragons, or five dots that represent love, money, prison, sin, and revenge.

Gang members usually traveled in groups of six or more, moving from state to state, staying in motels or rented apartments. They tended to victimize other Vietnamese Americans, especially targeting the elderly. Because of their experiences in Communist Vietnam, many Vietnamese Americans were distrustful of authority. They kept their savings and valuables not in a bank but in their house, leaving them vulnerable to burglary. When stealing from older Vietnamese Americans, gang members were fairly confident the theft would go unreported, since the victims were not comfortable dealing with the police. These gangs continue to be a blight on their communities in two ways—by preying on the elderly and by leading desperate young people into a life of crime.

• Study Questions •

I. What challenges did Vietnamese Americans with limited English skills face?

(continues on next page)

(continued from previous page)

2. What kept some Vietnamese Americans from seeking treatment for depression?

   ....

3. Why were some Vietnamese Americans still bitter about the U.S. military's 1973 withdrawal from Vietnam?

   ....

4. What happened to Vietnamese-American fishermen in Seadrift, Texas?

   ....

5. Why do some Vietnamese Americans join gangs?

   ....

8

The Changing Family

The Vietnamese long honored the family as the bedrock of their world. Their own sense of self came largely from their relationships with other family members. From their family, they derived the support they needed to survive difficult times. At the same time, they were obligated to help other family members and show them proper respect. In the United States, Vietnamese Americans tried to replicate their traditional family structure, but, as with every other aspect of their lives, family relationships underwent significant changes as Vietnamese Americans adapted to American life.

THE TRADITIONAL FAMILY

In Vietnam, families were strongly *patriarchal*, meaning that the father had authority over his wife and children. This family structure reflected Chinese values passed along to the Vietnamese during the period in which the Chinese ruled their lands. A

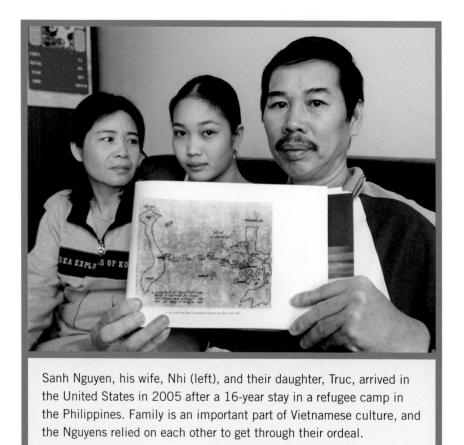

Sanh Nguyen, his wife, Nhi (left), and their daughter, Truc, arrived in the United States in 2005 after a 16-year stay in a refugee camp in the Philippines. Family is an important part of Vietnamese culture, and the Nguyens relied on each other to get through their ordeal.

good father demanded obedience and dealt out harsh discipline if he was defied. One middle-aged woman, who arrived in the United States in 1980, described her impressions of her father when she was a girl: "All of us children feared him. . . . We had to eat properly with chopsticks, and slowly, not fast. We had to speak properly, as girls do. And if we made a mistake, he would shout out, 'Ho! Attention! No more!' I feared him."[60]

Children were expected to obey and revere their parents. In Vietnamese thinking, children owed a great debt to their mothers and fathers for bringing them into the world. This debt could only be repaid through subservience and service. A man named Phuong Hoang recalled the sayings he was taught as a child so he would remember his duties within the family: "We grew up hearing proverbs that reminded us of our obligations: 'Fish without salt smells bad; children who talk back become bad.' To remember the role of our parents, we heard, 'when drinking water, remember our parents, who made that success possible.'"[61] Older siblings were also expected to care for and serve as role models for the younger children in the family.

Wives were supposed to defer to their husbands, but in Vietnamese society, their deference was not total. Traditionally, Vietnamese women had more freedom than women in some other Asian cultures. The Vietnamese respected strong women and told stories about them in history and legend. In both urban and rural areas, it was not unusual for women to work outside the house or to handle the household finances.

A NEW INDEPENDENCE

Even before the mass migration of Vietnamese to the United States, family roles were beginning to change. For instance, traditionally, parents had chosen wives and husbands for their children. By the twentieth century, however, it was common for young people to decide for themselves who they wanted to marry, as long as they paid heed to their parents' advice on the matter. In addition, women were growing more independent. One reason was women's literacy campaigns launched after 1945 by Vietnamese Communists. Literacy helped introduce women to more experiences outside the home.

Less beneficial were the changes brought by years of war and suffering. Women whose husbands were killed in battle were left alone to fend for their children. After Vietnam fell to Communist rule, many families were torn apart as fathers and husbands were sent off to reeducation camps. With no idea when their husbands might return, some women remarried. Often, tensions grew between children and their new stepfathers. The breakdown of family ties was augmented by the climate of terror. The Communists pressured children to spy on their parents and wives to spy on their husbands. Families fell apart as people feared their closest relatives might turn them over to the authorities.

IN AMERICA

The worst of such stresses were relieved when a family immigrated to the United States. Soon, however, people discovered that adjusting to American society created other threats to the traditional Vietnamese family. Perhaps the most jarring was the shift in the relationship between the young and the old.

In Vietnam, elders were held in high esteem. The young were not only expected to care for the old, but they were also supposed to follow the advice of their learned elders. The aged's years of experience in life yielded knowledge that young people respected and valued.

Often in the United States, the situation was turned on its head. The wisdom older people had accumulated in Vietnam no longer seemed to have much relevance. In America, certain practical skills, such as speaking English and being willing to learn new ways and customs, seemed more important. Most often, it was young people, not elders, who were able to accumulate the knowledge needed to get through life in their new land.

Adding to the elders' loss of status was their sense that they had become a burden to their families. In Vietnam, no one begrudged the money and time needed to care for the elderly. Instead, children learned early that caring for their parents was one of their most important roles in life. In America, however, every able-bodied adult in a family needed to go out to work to earn a living. Left alone day after day, some elders became painfully lonely. They resented their children, feeling they were not living up to their obligations to serve them in their old age.

Retaining cultural identity has been an ongoing problem for Vietnamese Americans. Here, Thi Hoa, who is dressed in traditional Vietnamese clothing, and her grandson Tran Quoc Viet wait for a bus in the Little Saigon district of Westminster, California.

Small children, especially those born in America, were not always taught to bow to older people and address them in ways that showed them proper respect. Even more devastating, some grandparents found themselves literally unable to communicate with their grandchildren, since they knew no English and their grandchildren never learned Vietnamese.

Younger family members in the United States often worked for years to bring their elders to live with them. In some cases, however, these reunions proved bittersweet. Older people felt isolated and depressed in a new world that confused them. Some came to regret leaving their home country. In the late 1980s, one such woman lamented her situation: "If it were peaceful, I would live in Vietnam. . . . I'd make a living selling rice paper or chicken and pigs. It's a more comfortable life."[62]

PARENTAL CONTROL

Tensions between elders and their adult offspring were mirrored in the relationships between these adults and their own children. Seeing the relative freedom of American children and adults, young Vietnamese Americans sometimes came to resent their parents' control over their lives. Le Van Hieu, who was 13 when he arrived in the United States, recounted his parents' rules for him throughout his teens:

> Our parents make . . . decisions for us: the classes we should take, our academic majors, even our schedules. Until the age of 21, I had a curfew. I had to be back home at midnight. What they want from us is to study, to concentrate on education, and not to take drugs or alcohol. They don't want us even to take a job. They would rather work overtime to let us study more. Our job is to get an education.[63]

Vietnamese-American parents, especially fathers, were apt to complain about American society and its corrupting influence over their children. They saw contemporary dress, television, and other aspects of American teenage life as eroding their children's respect for the family and submission to their authority. If their children disobeyed their wishes, they were likely to accuse them of thoughtless ingratitude.

For their own part, some Vietnamese-American children and teenagers complained that their parents expected too much. Their parents' emphasis on education put them under constant pressure, especially if they were not measuring up to their successful siblings. Some Vietnamese-American teens even felt their parents would be wise to emulate elements of American-style parenting. For instance, many wished their parents would talk over problems, instead of making decisions for them.

WORKING FOR THE FAMILY

Vietnamese-American teenagers also often questioned their father's control over the family's finances. Often, families insisted that teens not work, so they could concentrate on their schooling. On the other hand, if teenagers took part-time jobs to help out, they were generally expected to give their paychecks to their father. The coworker of one 17-year-old with a job at a fast-food restaurant called him stupid for surrendering his pay. The teen did not agree: "But I said that my dad gives me life and my family supports me. We all give ours [earnings] to the family and who needs it will have it. I don't think that I am stupid."[64]

Some teenagers balked at the old system, particularly when they began to want the luxuries that other American teens had. As one young man explained: "Now I need my money for my car, and for my dating, I tried to tell my father that this is how we do it in America, but I don't think he understands. He still thinks we are in Vietnam."[65]

Some parents took control over their teenagers' finances just to keep them from spending money like their peers. These parents were offended by the importance placed on buying material goods. They were also upset by the time teenagers devoted to their friends, time the parents felt was better spent with family. As one father in Oklahoma City explained:

> I love my children, but I do not always like what they are doing. My children want to spend less time with us and more time with their friends. They are not interested in their country's history, and they do not speak Vietnamese .... If they want to be like some Americans, that is all right, but not to be Vietnamese is not okay. They are too much like Americans and this distresses me.[66]

DATING AND MARRIAGE

Dating was another area in which parents and their children often disagreed. Traditionally in Vietnam, young people did not go on dates, and they never touched or kissed each other in public. Not surprisingly, some Vietnamese-American parents were very uncomfortable with American dating habits. Some forbade their children to date, particularly while they were still in school. As this father of a 19-year-old son understood, these strict parents could not always know what the children were doing: "I think that my son has dated, but he has not told me. He knows that I do not want him to date, but he is in the university and so he has a lot of his own time. . . . I am afraid that if he has a lot of dating he will not have good grades."[67]

Selecting marriage partners could also be a source of conflict. A few parents went so far as wanting to choose their children's spouses. Others expected to at least be consulted in the decision, and many made it clear they wanted their children to marry someone of Vietnamese ancestry. Some young people resisted this thinking, but others agreed that other Vietnamese Americans were the most suitable spouses. Hieu, a young woman married to a Vietnamese American, explained her choice: "Every one of my relatives has married a Vietnamese, and I prefer that too. We understand each other better, have the same culture and speak the same language."[68]

HUSBANDS AND WIVES

Perhaps more than any other family relationship, the bond between Vietnamese-American wives and husbands changed. For many men, these changes in the marriage dynamic seemed like a catastrophe. They missed the traditional family structure, in which the husband was fully in charge. On the other hand, although some women looked back on the traditional family with nostalgia, others enjoyed the new freedoms and opportunities they found in America.

Emigrating gave one refugee, who arrived in the United States in her 40s, a chance to escape a torturous marriage: "My parents chose a man for me whom I did not really want. . . . He never helped me with anything; he never took care of his children, and he never gave me any money. I feared him because he would bully me. . . . I like American ways and American people. I like the freedom that women have here."[69] This woman was so fed up with her husband that, when he wanted to follow her to the United States, she refused to be his sponsor.

The biggest change for most Vietnamese-American women was the chance to work outside the home. In Vietnam, women, especially those living in cities, often took jobs to help the family through a financial crisis or to save for a large purchase. In the United States, though, many more had to take full-time work, and these jobs were often menial and low-paying.

Nevertheless, many women liked the independence that came with earning money; they also enjoyed the contact they had with people outside their family. A woman in Southern California explained the satisfaction she felt from holding a job: "The new changes are good for me and for my family. I like helping pay the family expenses, and I think my husband is starting to accept this. My children like it, too, because we have more money for clothes and we are planning to buy a bigger house."[70]

Other women questioned whether the increased independence was worth the new tensions introduced into some marriages. One woman noted: "I think that money independence is hurting us. . . . This independence of the family is causing divorce which we did not have like this in Vietnam. I think that it is very bad."[71]

In truth, the divorce rate in Vietnam was traditionally very low. (Divorce carried such a stigma that a man was more likely to abandon his wife and children than to consent to a divorce.) Even in the United States, the rate of divorce among Vietnamese has remained relatively low. According to the 2000 census, about 4.1 percent of Vietnamese Americans 15 and older are divorced. This figure is less than half the percentage of divorcees in the total U.S. population (about 9.7 percent).

FINDING A BALANCE

A far less devastating consequence of changing gender roles was how Vietnamese-American women viewed housework. Women traditionally did all the work around the house. They were especially proud of the delicious, time-consuming meals they lovingly cooked for their families.

As wives took on full-time work, they increasingly looked for help from their husbands—sometimes, in vain. As one mother of seven explained: "Most of the time, my husband sits in his big chair and relaxes when he comes home from work. He helps me with some of the housework and sometimes cooking, but he is not very good. This is hard for him. It is also hard for me. I try to show him that he is still the head of the family and that his helping does not change that."[72] Like many Vietnamese-American women, this mother had to struggle to find a way to blend Vietnamese ideals about home life with American ideals about the workplace.

Another woman described her own balancing act optimistically: "Here in America, I live in two worlds. Outside the house, I am more American, a modern-day woman, an educated and professional woman. But I still have a role as a homemaker."[73] It is just this ability to blend familiar and unfamiliar ways that allowed many Vietnamese Americans to craft successful professional lives while preserving meaningful personal relationships.

• Study Questions •

1. Traditionally, who was the head of the Vietnamese family?

2. How did the Vietnam War affect family roles?

3. How were elders received in North America?

4. How did dating and marriage customs change for Vietnamese Americans in the United States?

5. What new freedoms did Vietnamese-American women enjoy?

9

Prominent Vietnamese Americans

The National Congress of Vietnamese Americans made this statement on the thirtieth anniversary of the fall of Saigon:

> Over the past 30 years, the majority of Vietnamese Americans came to the United States with nothing more than their internal desire to live free and productive lives. Today, members of this community are elected officials, business owners, sport stars and individuals helping to shape and defend the future of America. . . . The Vietnamese American community is no longer a community with a tragic history. It is a community rich in culture and heritage. Vietnamese Americans are modern-day pilgrims in a land of opportunities.[74]

Since they first arrived, Vietnamese Americans have had an important impact on American society, both collectively and as individuals. Indeed, today Vietnamese-American success stories abound, with people of talent and achievement excelling in just about every field of activity.

IN BUSINESS

Many Vietnamese Americans have become successful business people. One of the best-known Vietnamese-American entrepreneurs is Frank Jao. As the CEO (chief executive officer) of Bridgecreek Development Company, Jao has been instrumental in developing the Little Saigon district of Westminster, California. He has also served as the chairman of the board of the Vietnam Education Foundation, an organization established by Congress to build ties between the United States and Vietnam through student exchanges.

Another prominent business leader, Binh Nguyen, started surprisingly small. He opened his first restaurant in San Jose, California, in 1984. With only enough room for six diners at a time, it specialized in traditional Vietnamese beef noodle soup. Over the years, Nguyen added more dishes and opened more restaurants. Eventually, he began franchising Pho Hoa Noodle Soup restaurants in seven countries. There are now about 100 Pho Hoa restaurants throughout the world.

Hau Thai-Tang holds degrees in mechanical engineering and business—a perfect educational background for his job as the Director of Advanced Product Creation at the Ford Motor Company. While working at Ford, Thai-Tang has overseen the design and development of the Thunderbird and Mustang automobiles and the Windstar minivan.

Truong Dinh Tran is known both as a businessman and as a philanthropist. Before emigrating, Tran was the CEO and principal owner of the Vishipco Line, the largest shipping company in South Vietnam. His ships helped evacuate thousands after

Frank Jao, the CEO of Bridgecreek Development Company, has played a prominent role in the growth of Westminster, California's Little Saigon district. In addition, Jao has served as the chairman of the board of the Vietnam Education Foundation, a federal agency whose mission is to strengthen ties between the United States and Vietnam through educational exchanges in science and technology.

the fall of Saigon. Since arriving in the United States in 1975, he has operated a number of hotels, including Hotel Opera and Hotel Carter in New York City. After the terrorist attack on the city's World Trade Center in 2001, Tran donated $2 million to the American Red Cross's relief efforts.

Taryn Rose is the most prominent Vietnamese American to make it in the fashion industry. Before becoming a shoe designer in 1998, Rose graduated from medical school, where she trained to be an orthopedic surgeon. There, she saw patients with feet deformed by ill-fitting, high-heeled shoes. Rose decided customers deserved shoes that were both beautiful and comfortable. Although practical, her designs are highly fashionable and popular among celebrities. Sold in upscale stores throughout the country, Rose's shoes are also showcased in her own boutiques, located in New York, Beverly Hills, San Jose, and Las Vegas.

THE WORLD OF ENTERTAINMENT

A number of talented Vietnamese Americans have found success in Hollywood. Particularly recognizable to television viewers is Dustin Nguyen. In 1975, Nguyen arrived in the United States knowing only a few words of English. Twelve years later, at the age of 24, he was starring in the television series *21 Jump Street*. His own escape from Vietnam provided the basis for an episode titled "Christmas in Saigon." Nguyen has since been a regular on the syndicated series *V.I.P.* and appeared in the films *Heaven and Earth* (1993), *Hundred Percent* (1998), and *Little Fish* (2005).

Vietnamese-American actress Thuy Trang arrived in the United States in 1979, when she was six years old. Settling in California, she began to study kung fu and developed an interest in acting. Trang won the role as Trini Kwan (the "Yellow Ranger") in the popular children's television series *Mighty Morphin' Power Rangers* and also appeared in movies, such as

The Crow: City of Angels (1996) and *Spy Hard* (1996). Sadly, Trang's career was cut short in 2001, when she was killed in a car accident.

Several other Vietnamese-American entertainers are just beginning to make a name for themselves. They include model Navia Nguyen, who in 1997 became the first Asian American photographed for the *Sports Illustrated* swimsuit issue. She has since appeared in several films, including *Hitch* (2005) and *Memoirs of a Geisha* (2005). Up-and-comer Damien Nguyen garnered critical praise for the film *The Beautiful Country* (2005), in which he plays a young Asian-American man who journeys to Texas to find his American father. And comedian Dat Phan became nationally known when in 2003 he won *Last Comic Standing*, a televised competition to find the funniest new stand-up comic in the country.

The Bui brothers have found their calling behind the camera. Tony and Timothy Bui arrived in the United States when they were infants. Their father ran a video store in Sunnydale, California, and early on, the Buis developed a fascination with film, which they later combined with their interest in their home country. After visiting Vietnam several times, Tony Bui wrote and directed a short film *Yellow Lotus* (1995). His second movie, *Three Seasons* (1999), cowritten with Timothy, was the first American film shot in Vietnam. The two Buis also worked together on *Green Dragon* (2001), which they cowrote and Timothy directed. This feature tells the story of first-wave Vietnamese immigrants taken to Camp Pendleton, California, after escaping Vietnam. One of the lead actors in the film is the Buis' uncle, Don Duong, who has appeared in several other American films.

THE SPORTING LIFE

For years, Vietnamese Americans have been strong competitors in the sport of table tennis. The best known are Khoa Nguyen and Tawny Banh. Both were members of the U.S. tennis table teams that participated in the 2000 and 2004 Olympics.

Badminton player Howard Bach is another Vietnamese-American Olympian. After competing in the 2004 Olympics in Athens, Bach won the 2005 World Badminton Championship in men's doubles.

A few Vietnamese-American athletes have excelled in popular American sports. In 1994, Danny Graves was drafted by the Cleveland Indians, becoming the first Vietnamese American to play for a professional baseball team. He was later traded to the Cincinnati Reds and was a relief pitcher for the New York Mets in 2005 before returning to the Cleveland Indians in 2006.

In 1999, Dat Nguyen became the first Vietnamese-American professional football player. Although at five feet eleven, he is physically smaller than most players, Nguyen wowed fans during his college career at Texas A&M, setting several records. He was then drafted to play for the Dallas Cowboys. In his second season with the team, he was their starting middle linebacker and made the second-highest number of tackles of any Cowboy in a single season. In 2004, Nguyen was selected the Cowboys' defensive team captain but was forced to retire in 2006 due to a knee injury.

DELIVERING THE NEWS

Journalism is another field in which Vietnamese Americans have excelled. Some learned their craft while covering the Vietnam War. One such professional, photojournalist Nick Ut, was responsible for perhaps the most famous image of the war—a harrowing image of badly burned children running down a road. Now working for the Associated Press's Los Angeles bureau, Ut won the coveted Pulitzer Prize for that photograph.

Some Vietnamese print journalists work for mainstream newspapers and magazines. Others work for the many newspapers, journals, and radio and television stations that produce news specifically for the Vietnamese-American community. Among the latter, the best regarded is Yen Ngoc Do. With a few friends, Do founded *Nguoi Viet* in Orange

EUGENE H. TRINH: THE FIRST VIETNAMESE AMERICAN TO TRAVEL TO OUTER SPACE

The talents of physicist and astronaut Eugene H. Trinh have literally taken him sky high. Trinh was born in Saigon in 1950. His father, an engineer working for the United Nations, moved his family to Paris, France, when Trinh was a toddler. Educated in Paris public schools, Trinh moved to the United States in 1968 to continue his studies. In 1972, he received a bachelor's degree in mechanical engineering and applied physics at Columbia University. He later earned two master's and one doctorate at Yale University. Trinh emerged as an expert in fluid mechanics—the branch of physics that studies the motion of liquids and gases.

In 1981, the National Aeronautics and Space Administration (NASA) began flights using the space shuttle—a reusable vehicle on which scientists could perform experiments in space. Two years later, Trinh applied to work on the space shuttle program. He did not get an opportunity to go into space, until 1992, when he was accepted as a payload specialist on the crew of the space shuttle *Columbia*. Working 12-hour days onboard the shuttle was difficult, but Trihn was thrilled by the experience. As he recalled, "[It is] the best thing one can do . . . going around the earth, being able to look down at the ocean and the earth."[*]

After his space flight, Trinh continued to work at NASA. Trinh is now the director of the Physical Sciences Research Division in the Biological and Physical Research Enterprise. In this role, he oversees a program devoted to studying the biological, chemical, and physical effects of gravity. The program will help NASA develop technologies that will enable future human space exploration.

---

* Gale Research, "Eugene Huu-Chau Trinh," *Notable Asian Americans*. Reproduced in Biography Resource Center (Farmington Hills, Mich.: Thomson Gale, 2005).

County, California, in 1978. Working out of Do's garage, they produced a four-page weekly newspaper. Do not only edited

In 1992, Eugene Trinh became the first Vietnamese American to travel to outer space when he served as a payload specialist aboard the STS-50/United States Microgravity Lab-1 Space Shuttle. In 2005, Trinh was named the director of the NASA Management Office, at the Jet Propulsion Laboratory in Pasadena, California.

and designed the paper, but he also delivered copies door to door. Since its humble beginnings, *Nguoi Viet* has grown into an important voice for the Vietnamese-American community. With Do still as its editor, *Nguoi Viet* is now produced daily and has a circulation of about 16,000. Written in Vietnamese, *Nguoi Viet* delivers news from both the United States and Vietnam of particular interest to Vietnamese Americans. In 2003, Do launched *Nguoi Viet 2*. This English-language weekly provides news for younger Vietnamese Americans whose first language is English.

Vietnamese Americans are also prominent in broadcast journalism. One of the most notable is Betty Nguyen. Arriving in the United States in 1975, Nguyen grew up in Texas, where she began her career as an anchor and reporter for a Waco station. She later moved to Dallas to work at its CBS affiliate. While in Dallas, Nguyen covered the *Columbia* space shuttle disaster and the September 11 attacks and won a regional Emmy Award for "Outstanding Noon Newscast." In 2004, Nguyen became a national news anchor for CNN, at its world headquarters in Atlanta, Georgia. With her mother, Nguyen has also founded the charity Help the Hungry, which delivers medicine and supplies to impoverished Vietnamese villages.

TELLING STORIES

Many Vietnamese Americans have used the written word to tell of their struggles in both Vietnam and the United States. Initially, some writers, desperate to tell their stories, printed up their memoirs themselves to distribute to friends and relatives. More recently, a growing number of writers have had their works published by major American publishing houses. These memoirs include Andrew X. Pham's *Catfish and Mandala* (2000) and Kien Nguyen's *The Unwanted: A Memoir of Childhood* (2001).

Perhaps the best known Vietnamese-American memoirist is Le Ly Hayslip, who experienced the horrors of torture and rape during the Vietnam War. Escaping to the United States in

1970, Hayslip, with coauthor Jay Wurts, wrote about her past in *When Heaven and Earth Changed Places: A Vietnamese Woman's Journey from War to Peace* (1989). By focusing on a Vietnamese woman's experiences, the book was hailed for providing a perspective on the war that previously had been largely ignored. With her son James, Hayslip wrote a second memoir, *Child of War, Woman of Peace* (1993), which deals with her life in the United States, where she became an activist. Both of these memoirs provided the basis for director Oliver Stone's film *Heaven and Earth* (1993).

Vietnamese Americans have also explored their past and present through fiction. The first major Vietnamese-American novel published in the United States was *Monkey Bridge* (1997) by Lan Cao. The book tells the story of Mai Nguyen, a young woman who escapes Saigon with her widowed mother and creates a new life in Farmington, Connecticut. Other notable works of fiction by Vietnamese-American authors include the novels *The Gangster We Are All Looking For* (2003) by Le Thi Diem Thuy and *Grass Roof, Tin Roof* (2003) by Dao Strom, and the short story collection *We Should Never Meet* (2004) by Aimee Phan.

SERVING THE PUBLIC

In the early years of Vietnamese immigration, few Vietnamese Americans were involved in U.S. politics. Some remembered terrible experiences with government officials in Vietnam, so politics held little appeal for them. In addition, most were too busy building their lives and raising their families.

More recently, however, Vietnamese Americans have begun to move into the political arena. Leading the way was Tony Quang Lam. In 1992, he became the first Vietnamese American to be elected to public office. For 10 years, he served on the city council of Westminster, California. During his tenure, he helped register thousands of Vietnamese

In 2004, Van Tran became the first Vietnamese American elected to the California State Assembly when he won the right to represent the 68th District in Orange County. Born in Saigon, Tran moved with his family to the United States in 1975.

Americans to vote. He also encouraged the development of Westminster's Little Saigon before his retirement from the council in 2002.

In Maryland, Nguyen Minh Chau has served four terms as a member of the Garrett Park Town Council, making her the first female Vietnamese-American elected official. In addition to her political career, Chau has worked with a number of charitable and political organizations, including the Organization of Pan-Asian American Women. In 2002, Chau made an unsuccessful bid for a seat in Maryland's House of Delegates.

Two other Vietnamese-American politicians have succeeded in winning elections for seats in state legislative bodies, however.

In 2004, Hubert Vo, a successful businessman, was elected to the Texas House of Representatives. In the same year, Van Tran, a city councilman for Garden Grove, California, became a member of that state's assembly. After his election, Van Tran explained his situation: "[I have] a unique responsibility by virtue of the fact that I'm a Vietnamese American but . . . I have to represent everyone equally and I intend to do that."[75]

EDUCATING OTHERS

Given their respect for education, it is not surprising that many Vietnamese Americans have devoted their lives to teaching. At the university level, Vietnamese-American scholars include Chi Van Dang, vice dean for research at Johns Hopkins University School of Medicine; Yen Le Espiritu, professor of Ethnic Studies at the University of California, San Diego; and Chuong Hoang Chung, professor of Asian American Studies at City College of San Francisco and founder of the first Vietnamese-American Studies Program in the United States at San Francisco State University.

Vietnamese-American teachers are also found throughout the American elementary and secondary school system. Perhaps the best known is Huong Tran Nguyen, who in 1994 was chosen from 5,000 nominees as America's Outstanding Teacher. Nguyen came to the United States as a student in 1971, while the Vietnam War was still raging. She struggled through her studies at San Diego State University and because English was not her native language, one of her instructors told her, "you may never be a teacher of the same caliber as your . . . classmates. You must accept that as a fact."[76] Nguyen refused to accept this "fact," and instead devoted herself to becoming the best teacher she could, using her own difficulties in the classroom to inspire others. As she explained, "I serve as a role model for all students, particularly for language-minority students, who may have been socialized to think and to accept that the only work they could obtain are minimum-salaried jobs. I see them as potential leaders of tomorrow."[77]

• Study Questions •

1. Why did Vietnamese-American businessman Truong Dinh Tran donate $2 million to the Red Cross?

2. On what television show did actor Dustin Nguyen first find fame?

3. In what sport did Khoa Nguyen and Tawny Banh compete in the 2004 Olympics?

4. Who was the first Vietnamese American to play professional football?

5. What network does broadcast journalist Betty Nguyen work for?

6. Who was the first Vietnamese American elected to public office?

10

At Home in Two Countries

While touring the United States in 2005, Vietnamese Prime Minister Phan Van Khai made the following comments about Vietnam and its relationship to the United States: "[Vietnam has] a population of 80 million people, which means a huge market for American businesses. They are now working very hard to achieve the goal of building Vietnam into a strong country with wealthy people and a democratic and advanced society."[78] Vietnam is still a Communist country, but as Khai's words suggest, it is rapidly changing—economically, socially, and politically—and instrumental in these changes are Vietnamese Americans.

RENEWED RELATIONS

Since 1994, the relationship between the United States and Vietnam has shifted dramatically. At the end of the Vietnam War, the United States had instituted a trade *embargo*—that is,

In 1994, the United States lifted its trade embargo with Vietnam, and in 2001 the two nations signed the Vietnam–U.S. Trade Agreement, which opened their markets and reduced tariffs. American companies such as Compaq have benefited from this open market and have actively sought to expand their presence in Vietnam. Pictured here is a cyclist driving past an advertisement for Compaq computers in Hanoi.

it refused to trade goods with Communist Vietnam. By the late 1980s, the embargo, combined with the policies of the Vietnamese government, had all but destroyed the country's economy. Adding to the crisis, in 1991 Vietnam lost the substantial aid it received from the Soviet Union when that country's government dissolved.

In desperation, some Vietnamese officials moved to reform the nation's economy. Among their goals was opening trade with the West and attracting foreign investors. A boon to this goal came in 1994, when the United States lifted its trade embargo. The next year, the United States restored diplomatic relations with Vietnam.

This was important news for Vietnamese Americans. Although they were thousands of miles away, many had retained close ties to Vietnam. These ties were both financial, as Vietnamese Americans sent money to relatives left behind, and emotional, as they cherished their bittersweet memories of Vietnam. The normalization of relations with Vietnam meant that these ties could become even closer. For the first time, Vietnamese Americans could visit their homeland without fear of reprisals from or imprisonment by the Communist government.

VISITING HOME

Many Vietnamese Americans were eager to visit their homeland, but when they traveled there, they were often stunned by what they saw. For some, years of romanticizing Vietnamese life left them with unrealistic expectations. One woman described her disappointment: "I visited my ancestral home. I remembered it as big. Now the patio and the gate were gone, the trees were dead, and the paint was faded. It was dirty. When I saw the house, I just felt empty."[79]

Others felt shock at how much decay and destruction had set in after two decades of repressive Communist rule. After visiting Vietnam with her mother, Duong Thi Chi recalled her impressions: "After one week in Hanoi, [my mother] couldn't stand it, staying with relatives, seeing them struggle, seeing a broken-down Hanoi, not the beautiful city of her youth. She changed her ticket and left soon after. All of us were deeply disappointed and do not expect to return again."[80]

The attitude of the Vietnamese themselves also left some Vietnamese-American visitors bitter. Some Vietnamese, particularly officials, were openly hostile to these tourists. Businessman Dom Lam remembered his first trip to Vietnam, in 1994: "[T]he immigration officer at the airport gave me such a hard time because I didn't put a $10 bill in my passport. People then didn't trust [us]. They were envious of us, our overseas education, our expat salaries."[81]

THE VIET KIEU

More recently, the Vietnamese have been far more welcoming to the *Viet Kieu,* as Vietnamese living overseas are called. Many Vietnamese officials were at first suspicious of dealing with Westerners, fearing that they might try to subvert the Communist party's control. The benefits of foreign trade and investment were so great, however, that they soon set aside these concerns.

During the first years of the twenty-first century, trade between the United States and Vietnam skyrocketed. By 2004, this trade amounted to $7 billion, making the United States Vietnam's top trading partner. The benefits for the Vietnamese are most obvious in Ho Chi Minh City (formerly Saigon), where the bulk of American *capital* is spent. The average income per person in this city is four times the national average.

This booming trade is not only changing Vietnam. It is also changing the Vietnamese-American community. Knowing both Vietnamese and American customs, the American Viet Kieu are essential to integrating American businesses into the soaring Vietnamese economy. For many Vietnamese-American businesspeople, working in Vietnam is as personally satisfying as it is lucrative. As Nguyen Duy Binh, the manager of Federal Express in Vietnam, explained: "It's very rewarding, because you have a chance to have two countries to come home to. Part of me is U.S., and part of me is Vietnamese."[82]

RETURNING TO VIETNAM

Vietnamese Americans are visiting Vietnam increasingly as tourists. Since the mid-1990s, Vietnam has vastly improved its tourism industry. With plans for building luxury hotels and theme parks, Vietnam now attracts 3 million tourists a year. After Japan, the United States sends the largest number of tourists there.

Generally, Vietnamese Americans are finding Vietnam much more inviting than they were only a few years ago. Some are so pleased with the way of life there that they are taking advantage of a Vietnamese law, instituted in 2001, that allows foreigners to own property in Vietnam. Several American companies are working with Vietnamese construction firms to build houses specifically for Vietnamese-American buyers.

The vision of one developer, Paul Hoang of San Jose, illustrates the vital role of the Viet Kieu in Vietnam business. In Vietnamese cities, homes are often multistoried structures built close to the street. Knowing the tastes of Vietnamese Americans, Hoang instead offers his customers housing designs commonly found in California suburbs, including extras such as front gardens, swimming pools, tennis courts, and picture windows. Some Vietnamese Americans are buying homes in Vietnam as investments, but many plan to retire there. As Hoang explains, "I'm building for the older people, like my parents. After they work in the U.S. for so many years, they get tired and want to come back and have an easy life. Some of them complain they don't have enough money to retire in the U.S. They can have a very good life here."[83]

Some people, such as Nguyen Duy Binh, see investing in houses in Vietnam as good for their old homeland: "All the Vietnamese Americans I know have always wanted to come back and do something for their country. Viet Kieu investment is growing, and economic growth will help uplift the people of Vietnam."[84]

FIGHTING COMMUNISM

Not all Vietnamese Americans who are investing in Vietnam are so eager to admit it. They do not want to attract the scorn of a minority of Vietnamese Americans who fiercely oppose the new economic relationship between the United States and Communist Vietnam. Many were reeducation camp prisoners who were persecuted by the Communist regime, an experience that made them strongly anti-Communist.

One of the most important political issues among Vietnamese Americans is their opposition to Vietnam's Communist government. Some Vietnamese Americans protested Vietnam Prime Minister Phan Van Khai's visit to the United States in June 2005, including this woman in Westminster, California, who is striking the Communist leader's portrait.

Increasingly, Vietnamese Americans are becoming involved in political issues. According to the 2000 U.S. census, about 68 percent are U.S. citizens, the second-largest percentage (after Filipinos) of any other Asian-American group. Many are also registered voters, the majority of whom are aligned with the Republican Party.

The anti-Communists are still the most vocal political faction in the Vietnamese-American community. They often stage protests to speak out against actions perceived as helping to support the Communists in Vietnam. For instance, several hundred Vietnamese Americans protested against President

George W. Bush's meeting with Phan Van Khai in June 2005. The meeting marked the first time a Vietnamese leader was welcomed inside the White House since the end of the Vietnam War. Although Bush pledged to support Vietnam's economic reforms and promised to visit Vietnam the following year, Vietnamese-American demonstrators, many from as far away as California, gathered nearby, shouting slogans such as "Down with Communism." Despite the anti-Communist faction's opposition to Bush's Vietnam policy, it was generally supportive of his 2004 reelection bid, in large part because of the opposition to the Vietnam War voiced by Bush's Democratic rival Senator John Kerry in the 1970s.

Although some Vietnamese-American political activists still oppose all U.S. dealings with the Vietnamese government, others feel that continued relations between the two countries is inevitable. As Phu Nguyen, president of the Vietnamese Veterans Association of San Francisco, explained: "All this commerce brings riches to only the Communist Party members. But it's useless to protest it. Everybody wants to do business with Vietnam now. We can't stop that anymore."[85]

And some see a ray of hope in the surging Vietnamese economy. According to Dam Nguyen, president of the Vietnamese American Committee of Northern California, exposure to the American economic and political system could sow the seeds of revolution in Vietnam: "I strongly believe things will change in the near future. People in this country are rising up in protest. They understand that democracy is the better way."[86]

Although still important in Vietnamese-American life, the anti-Communist faction is dominated by older people. Younger activists tend to be less interested in Vietnam's politics. Instead, they are more focused on exerting influence over the American political scene in ways that can help Vietnamese Americans.

LOOKING FORWARD

On April 30, 2005, the thoughts of all Vietnamese Americans—young and old, Vietnamese natives and American-born—were on their homeland. That day marked the thirtieth anniversary of the fall of Saigon, and thus also the thirtieth anniversary of the beginning of the Vietnamese-American community in the United States.

In *USA Today*, short story writer Aimee Phan offered her own reflections on the anniversary, noting how, over the years, its meaning has changed for Vietnamese Americans: "What initially consisted of bitter recollection of the Communist occupation has slowly evolved into a commemoration of lost relatives

Tracing Your Roots

VALUABLE RESOURCES THAT CAN HELP REVEAL YOUR LINEAGE

If you are a Vietnamese American, tracing your ancestry can be fascinating and fun. By discovering your Vietnamese roots, you can learn more about your family, including why they came to the United States and what their life was like in the old country.

The best place to start is at home. Explain to your parents that you want to study your ancestry. Ask them to tell you everything they know about their parents, their parent's parents, and so on. Be sure to take careful notes. Write down your ancestors' names, birth and death dates, and, if possible, where they lived in Vietnam. To make your research more complete, ask your parents if they have any photographs of these people.

Next, interview other relatives you know—grandparents, aunts, uncles, cousins, or any other family members. They might be able to fill in gaps in the information your parents have given you.

and friends, nostalgia for the old country and a determination to move beyond the refugee label."[87]

Phan also acknowledged that, although still a sober occasion, this anniversary offered today's Vietnamese Americans a reason to hope for the future:

> While April 30, 1975, marked the end of the Vietnam my family knew, the day this year opens up the possibility of a new Vietnam. It isn't the country my parents' generation hoped would emerge out of the war. Far from it. But it isn't as terrible now as it once was. The country is healing, and so, eventually, will its people, no matter where they live.[88]

You might also have relatives in Vietnam who you could write to with questions. If you do not know Vietnamese, seek out a friend or relative who does, and ask them to translate your letter.

Also, if a family member is planning to go to Vietnam, you might ask them to help with your research. If they visit some of your Vietnamese relatives, for instance, they could pass along a list of questions from you.

Based on all your research, you may want to put together a pedigree chart, also known as a family tree. This is a diagram with the names of your ancestors and their birth and death dates, with lines connecting each generation.

For further help in tracing your roots and in making a pedigree chart, try consulting the following resources:

- National Genealogical Society: www.ngsgenealogy.org
- Ancestors in the Americas: www.cetel.org
- Family Search: www.familysearch.org
- Renick, Barbara. *Genealogy 101: How to Trace Your Family's History and Heritage.* Nashville, Tenn.: Rutledge Hill Press, 2003.

• Study Questions •

1. When did the United States restore diplomatic relations with Vietnam?

2. Which country is Vietnam's biggest trading partner?

3. What is Ho Chi Minh City?

4. Why are some Vietnamese Americans buying property in Vietnam?

5. Why did Vietnamese Americans object to the 2005 meeting between President George W. Bush and Vietnamese Prime Minister Phan Van Khai?

Chronology

1973 The United States signs a cease-fire with South Vietnam and North Vietnam, marking the end of U.S. involvement in the Vietnam War.

1975 The South Vietnamese government falls to North Vietnam; hundreds of thousands of South Vietnamese flee the country; congress passes the Indochina Migration and Refugee Act.

1978 *Nguoi Viet*, the first newspaper for Vietnamese Americans, starts publication; the mass exodus of "boat people" from Vietnam begins.

1979 Two men are killed in a violent confrontation involving Vietnamese-American fishermen in Seadrift, Texas.

1980 Congress passes the Refugee Act to enact the United Nations' Orderly Departure Program.

1987 Congress passes the Amerasian Homecoming Act.

1989 The United Nations develops the Comprehensive Plan of Action to discourage emigration from Indochina.

1990 The first former reeducation camp prisoners enter the United States under the State Department's Humanitarian Operation.

1992 Tony Quang Lam joins the city council of Westminster, California, and becomes the first Vietnamese American to hold elected public office.

1994 The United States lifts its trade embargo against Vietnam.

1995 The United States restores diplomatic relations with Vietnam.

1996 The last Vietnamese refugee camps in Asia are closed.

1998 *Monkey Bridge* by Lan Cao becomes the first major novel by a Vietnamese American published in the United States.

2000 The U.S. Census Bureau finds 1,122,528 people of Vietnamese ancestry living in the United States.

2001 A Vietnamese law allows foreigners to own property in Vietnam, prompting some

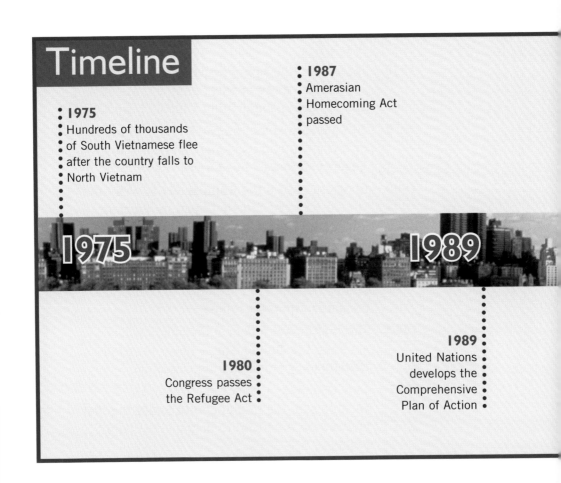

Timeline

1987
Amerasian
Homecoming Act
passed

1975
Hundreds of thousands
of South Vietnamese flee
after the country falls to
North Vietnam

1975   1989

1980
Congress passes
the Refugee Act

1989
United Nations
develops the
Comprehensive
Plan of Action

Vietnamese Americans to purchase homes there.

2004 Vietnamese Americans Hubert Vo of Texas and Van Tran of California are elected to their states' legislatures.

2005 Prime Minister Phan Van Khai of Vietnam meets with President George W. Bush in Washington, D.C., inciting protests by some Vietnamese-American groups. Hurricane Katrina destroys the livelihoods of many Vietnamese-American fishermen and shrimpers on the Gulf Coast.

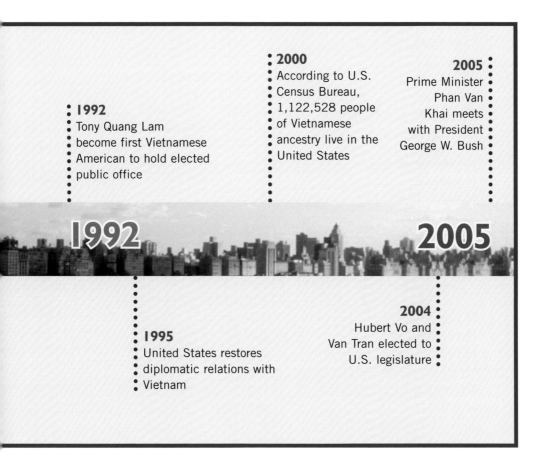

2000
According to U.S. Census Bureau, 1,122,528 people of Vietnamese ancestry live in the United States

2005
Prime Minister Phan Van Khai meets with President George W. Bush

1992
Tony Quang Lam become first Vietnamese American to hold elected public office

1992

2005

1995
United States restores diplomatic relations with Vietnam

2004
Hubert Vo and Van Tran elected to U.S. legislature

Notes

Chapter 1

1. Jade Ngoc Quang Huynh, *South Wind Changing* (Saint Paul, Minn.: Graywolf Press, 1994), 280.
2. Ibid., 6.
3. Ibid., 14.
4. Ibid., 275.
5. Ibid., 282.
6. Ibid.
7. Ibid., 283.
8. Ibid., 285.
9. Ibid., 283–284.
10. Ibid., 284.
11. Ibid., 288.
12. Ibid.
13. Ibid,. 289.
14. Ibid., 289–290.
15. Ibid., 302.
16. Ibid.

Chapter 2

17. James M. Freeman, *Hearts of Sorrow: Vietnamese-American Lives* (Stanford, Calif.: Stanford University Press, 1989), 115.
18. Ibid., 82–83.
19. Ibid., 121.
20. Ibid., 153.

Chapter 3

21. Ibid., 204.
22. Paul James Rutledge, *The Vietnamese Experience in America* (Bloomington: Indiana University Press, 1992), 21.

23. Ibid., 21–22.
24. Ibid., 17.
25. James M. Freeman, *Changing Identities: Vietnamese Americans, 1975–1995* (Boston: Allyn and Bacon, 1995), 47.

Chapter 4

26. Rutledge, *The Vietnamese Experience*, 22.
27. Ibid.
28. Freeman, *Changing Identities*, 62–63.
29. Ibid., 23.
30. Rutledge, *The Vietnamese Experience*, 26.
31. Freeman, *Changing Identities*, 25.
32. Ibid., 33.
33. Ibid., 37.
34. Rutledge, *The Vietnamese Experience*, 27.

Chapter 5

35. Rutledge, *The Vietnamese Experience*, 88–89.
36. Ibid., 79.
37. Ibid., 84.
38. Ibid., 78.
39. Rutledge, *The Vietnamese Experience*, 97.
40. Ibid., 116.
41. Ibid., 46.
42. Ibid., 45.
43. Ibid., 93.

Chapter 6

44. Freeman, *Changing Identities,* 73.
45. Ibid., 61.
46. Ibid., 12.

Chapter 7

47. Ibid., 102.
48. Ibid., 96.
49. Freeman, *Changing Identities,* 84.
50. Rutledge, *The Vietnamese Experience,* 92.
51. Freeman, *Changing Identities,* 84.
52. Rutledge, *The Vietnamese Experience,* 95.
53. Freeman, *Changing Identities,* 96.
54. Rutledge, *The Vietnamese Experience,* 105–106.
55. Freeman, *Changing Identities,* 64.
56. Ibid., 65.
57. Ibid., 7.
58. Rutledge, *The Vietnamese Experience,* 43–44.
59. Ibid., 108.

Chapter 8

60. Freeman, *Changing Identities,* 90.
61. Ibid., 88–89.
62. Ibid., 105.
63. Ibid., 81.
64. Rutledge, *The Vietnamese Experience,* 85.
65. Ibid,. 122.
66. Ibid., 104.
67. Ibid., 131.
68. Freeman, *Changing Identities,* 102.
69. Ibid., 98–99.

70. Rutledge, *The Vietnamese Experience,* 126.
71. Ibid.
72. Ibid., 125.
73. Freeman, *Changing Identities,* 100.

Chapter 9

74. National Congress of Vietnamese Americans, "NCVA Interviews on NPR's 'Talk of the Nation' and CNN International." April 27, 2005 press release. Available online at *www.ncva-online.org/archive/pr_042705_NPR_CNN_Interviews.shtml.*
75. Ben Fox, "First Vietnamese-American Lawmaker Is Object of Pride and Threats," November 3, 2004. Available online at *www.sfgate.com/cgi-bin/article.cgi?f=news/archive/2004/11/03/politics1945EST0500.DTL.*
76. "United States' Teacher of the Year in 1994." Available online at *www.ampact.net/nguyenth.htm.*
77. Ibid.

Chapter 10

78. Farah Stockman, "Bush Hosts, Praises Vietnamese Leader," *Boston Globe,* June 22, 2005.
79. Freeman, *Changing Identities,* 122.
80. Ibid., 123.
81. Sheridan Prasso, "Back to Vietnam," *Fortune,* April 4, 2005, 72.
82. Ibid.
83. Ibid.
84. Ibid.
85. K. Oanh Ha, "United Airlines Flight to Vietnam to Make

History," *San Jose Mercury News*, December 7, 2004.

86. Cicero A. Estrella, "The Fall of Saigon," *San Francisco Chronicle*, April 30, 2005.

87. Aimee Phan, "30 Years After Fall of Saigon, A Whole New

Perspective," *USA Today*, April 28, 2005.

88. Ibid.

Glossary

Amerasian The child of an American man, especially a U.S. soldier, and an Asian woman.

boat people Poor immigrants who flee their country in makeshift boats; most commonly used to describe the some 500,000 Vietnamese who escaped Vietnam by boat in the late 1970s and 1980s.

capital Money used to start a business.

dispersal policy U.S. government policy inaugurated in 1975 that sought to resettle recent Vietnamese immigrants throughout the country.

embargo Prohibition by one country's government on trade with a foreign nation.

entrepreneur A person who founds and operates a business.

ideology Ideas that form the basis of a political, economic, or other type of system.

immigrant A person who leaves his or her country and permanently resettles in another.

mutual assistance associations Organizations established by people in a group to help others in the group, such as organizations created by Vietnamese Americans to aid other Vietnamese Americans.

patriarchal Regarding a family or social system in which power is held primarily by men.

reeducation camps Prison camps to which a repressive government sends its political enemies.

refugee A person who flees his or her country, usually to escape political or religious persecution.

sponsor A person or group who agreed to provide housing, food, and other necessities for Vietnamese immigrants until they became financially self sufficient.

Viet Cong Rebel forces in South Vietnam who sided with the North Vietnamese Communists in the Vietnam War.

Viet Kieu Vietnamese people living outside of Vietnam.

Bibliography

Avakian, Monique. *Atlas of Asian-American History*. New York: Facts on File, 2002.

Cargill, Mary Terrell, and Jade Quang Huynh, eds. *Voices of the Vietnamese Boat People: Nineteen Narratives of Escape and Survival*. Jefferson, N.C.: McFarland & Company, 2000.

Do, Hien Duc. *The Vietnamese Americans*. Westport, Conn.: Greenwood Press, 1999.

Estrella, Cicero A. "The Fall of Saigon." *San Francisco Chronicle*, April 30, 2005.

Freeman, James M. *Changing Identities: Vietnamese Americans, 1975–1995*. Needham Heights, Mass.: Allyn and Bacon, 1995.

———. *Hearts of Sorrow: Vietnamese-American Lives*. Stanford, Calif.: Stanford University Press, 1989.

Ha, K. Oanh. "United Airlines Flight to Vietnam to Make History." *San Jose Mercury News*, December 7, 2004.

Hedgpeth, Dana. "A Family Business Beached." *Washington* Post, September 6, 2005.

Huynh, Jade Ngoc Quang. *South Wind Changing*. Saint Paul, Minn.: Graywolf Press, 1994.

Novas, Himilce, and Lan Cao, with Rosemary Silva. *Everything You Need to Know About Asian-American History*. 2004 Edition. New York: Plume, 2004.

Phan, Aimee. "30 Years After Fall of Saigon, A Whole New Perspective." *USA Today*, April 28, 2005.

Prasso, Sheridan. "Back to Vietnam." *Fortune*, April 4, 2005, 72–80.

Reeves, Terrance J., and Claudette E. Bennett. *We the People: Asians in the United States*. Washington, D.C.: U.S. Department of Commerce, 2004.

Rutledge, Paul James. *The Vietnamese Experience in America*. Bloomington: Indiana University Press, 1992.

Stockman, Farah. "Bush Hosts, Praises Vietnamese Leader." *Boston Globe*, June 22, 2005.

Tran, De, Andrew Lam, and Hai Dai Nguyen, eds. *Once Upon a Dream: The Vietnamese-American Experience.* Kansas City, Mo.: Andrews and McMeel. 1995.

Zhou, Min, and Carl L. Bankston III. *Growing Up American: How Vietnamese Children Adapt to Life in the United States.* New York: Russell Sage Foundation, 1998.

Further Reading

BOOKS

Caputo, Philip. *10,000 Days of Thunder: A History of the Vietnam War.* New York: Atheneum, 2005.

Cargill, Mary Terrell, and Jade Quang Huynh, eds. *Voices of the Vietnamese Boat People: Nineteen Narratives of Escape and Survival.* Jefferson, N.C.: McFarland & Company, 2000.

Coleman, Lori. *Vietnamese in America.* Minneapolis: Lerner Publications, 2005.

Gavin, Philip. *The Fall of Vietnam.* San Diego, Calif.: Lucent Books, 2003.

Parker, Edward. *Vietnam.* New York: Facts on File, 2005.

Springstubb, Tricia. *The Vietnamese Americans.* San Diego, Calif.: Lucent Books, 2002.

Warren, Andrea. *Escape from Saigon: How a Vietnam War Orphan Became an American Boy.* New York: Farrar, Straus and Giroux, 2004.

WEB SITES

Vietnam: Journeys of Body, Mind & Spirit
www.amnh.org/exhibitions/vietnam
> Based on an exhibit cosponsored by the Vietnam Museum of Ethnology, this site offers essays and videos about modern Vietnamese culture.

The Kim Foundation International
www.kimfoundation.com/en
> This site recounts the story of Vietnam War victim Phan Thi Kim Phuc and her efforts to help children injured by war.

National Congress of Vietnamese Americans
www.ncvaonline.org.
> The leading advocacy organization for Vietnamese Americans; the NCVA's Web site provides information about social, cultural, and economic issues of concern to Vietnamese Americans.

Nguoi Viet Online
www.nguoi-viet.com/nv2default.asp
> Here readers can find articles in English from Nguoi Viet, the United States's oldest Vietnamese-American newspaper.

Vietnamese American National Gala
www.vangusa.org
> On its official site, the Vietnamese American National Gala provides biographies of past winners of its coveted Golden Torch Award for outstanding contributions to the Vietnamese-American community.

Picture Credits

Index

About the Contributors

Series Editor **Robert D. Johnston** is associate professor and director of the Teaching of History Program in the Department of History at the University of Illinois at Chicago. He is the author of *The Making of America: The History of the United States from 1492 to the Present*, a middle school textbook that received a *School Library Journal* Best Book of the Year Award. He is currently working on a history of vaccine controversies in American history, to be published by Oxford University Press.

Liz Sonneborn is a writer, living in Brooklyn, New York. A graduate of Swarthmore College, she has written more than 50 books for children and adults, including *The German Americans*, *The American West*, *A to Z of American Women in the Performing Arts*, and *The New York Public Library's Amazing Native American History*, winner of a 2000 Parent's Choice Award.

In the late 1970s, Sonneborn was a high school student in Nashville, Tennessee, where many of her friends were recent immigrants from Vietnam. "I often asked my Vietnamese friends about their war experiences and their journeys to the United States," Sonneborn recalls. "They would humor me a little, but they didn't want to dwell on the past. They wanted to talk about math problems, television shows, college applications, and most of all what they hoped to be doing after high school. I was amazed at their enthusiasm for the future, given the trauma they'd lived through. They were by far the most resilient people I've ever met."